Lusting

After

Love

Lusting After Love

Caught In The Bright Lights of Darkness

Amanda Johnston

Dedication

First I want to dedicate this to my family who even though
I did not see it at the time always had my best interest at heart.
They never gave up hope that I would see my self-worth
and become the amazing person they saw in me.
A special thank you to my Granny, Aunt B and Aunt Peggy,
Grandma and Grandpa. Without your help this book
wouldn't have been published.
Second, to my husband who helped me out of
a very dark time in my life and has given me
my amazing daughter and son.
To my kids and all the sons and daughters
out there, may you never have to go down my path
but learn from my story instead.
Thirdly, to the Lord, although I did not see it at the time,
He was watching over me as I went through the darkest times
of my life, and He bought me out. He has given me this story to share
in hopes to reach those who He knows need to hear.
And lastly to those who feel like life isn't worth it,
that there's no other option and that they can't do any better
for themselves than what they are doing...
it's not true! You can still have an amazing life,
so please don't give up hope.

Table of Contents

Introduction

As I sit here a few weeks away from giving birth to our beautiful daughter, I cannot help but think about life. I have learned that the third trimester leads to many sleepless nights spent thinking about life, the coming future and wondering how my husband can fall asleep so quickly and so peacefully.

My precious daughter will be coming into the world in the middle of a global pandemic, and no one really knows when things will get back to some sort of normalcy. Who really knows what normal is anyway? Will her idea of normal be anything like what my idea of normal was as a child?

The world has changed so much, and we all go through things in our own lives that shape our reality. Will she choose differently than I did, and grow up strong and determined to not let anyone lead her astray? I pray she will look back on her childhood as fondly as I do mine.

I grew up in a very loving military Christian family. My parents truly made the best of what we had, and they did their best to never let us kids see when there were money or relationship struggles. They did all they could to give me and my sisters the world. I hope I can do this for my child, too, and that she will never feel when I'm stressed or depressed, and will always know that she is loved.

I know there's only so much I can do to protect her, and it only makes me worry more about her when she goes from a teenager to an adult. This world can eat you up without you even knowing it. That's exactly what happened to me, no matter how hard my parents tried to protect me. It seemed the harder they tried, the more I rebelled, which pulled me into a darkness and evil I never knew existed, and it almost destroyed me.

I don't know where I put God during all this rebellion, but I wasn't listening to Him either. I abandoned Him and all I had been taught. And He watched from afar, but I know He never let me go. I had a lesson to learn… the hard way.

My choices left me far away from everything I knew to be right. And because of those choices and ignoring all the red flags that were obvious to so many, I went through hell on earth, and it left me with unimaginable scars on my heart. It changed the way I innocently viewed a world that no longer existed for me.

No one wanted this for me, but perhaps it happened so that my daughter would never have to experience it. Or maybe, just maybe, my story might help others who chose a similar path and are now going through their own hell and regret, and they think there is no way out. But they are wrong.

I have things in my past that my closest friends would never guess… but then who doesn't have skeletons in their closets? For the longest time these experiences left me so broken, I became numb to the idea that I could love and be loved in return. I allowed myself to go down a very dark path, even knowing how wrong it was.

I've spent years trying to block out these memories, clinging to the hope that I will one day come to love myself like I should, and that others would love me too. I got to a point where I wasn't sure if I was trying to hide from myself or from my family and friends, but I know that I am tired of all the secrets and lies. It's time for me to come out of the closet and come clean!

What you are about to read is true. This is the story of how someone can survive extreme loneliness while walking through the darkness of hell, yet still able to thrive long after and have the life that was always meant to be theirs.

Only you know what happens behind closed doors! And

though I will never forget those dark days, I will always be grateful that I wasn't too damaged to forgive myself, and to put myself back together again.

My hope is that by sharing my story it will help bring someone else out of a very dark and dangerous situation and into the light where they can live and love as they were always meant to do.

1

Sweet Beginnings

Let me just start my story by saying there was absolutely no excuse for my rebellion that swept over me as a senior in high school. I was dearly loved by the wonderful parents God had given me. They raised me under Biblical words and truths, so I knew better.

I was a good girl. I knew right from wrong, and good from bad, but I did it anyway. Maybe I wasn't as grounded in my spiritual beliefs as I thought, or maybe I unknowingly left a door open for Satan to move in. I don't know, but I was on my way into a darkness I never knew before and hopefully never would again.

I was 17 years old in my senior year of high school in 2006, and my life could not have been better. I was active in the FFA, a student athlete, active in the school's religious group, in the top seventy-five students of my class, and about to celebrate my third anniversary with Justin, my high school sweetheart.

I never went through any type of rebellion, and never really got into any trouble, even as a teenager. My parents were teenagers when they had me, so you'd think my life would have been harder. Yet, I didn't come from a broken home, and my parents both worked hard to keep my sisters and me happy while their marriage thrived.

My dad was an honorable military man who worked full-time at a civilian job during the week, and one weekend a month he was on base fulfilling his military duty. My mom was a stay-at-home mom, raising us kids and was one of my closest friends, and I trusted her with everything.

While I wasn't the most popular girl in school, I had plenty of great friends to share my world. My close-knit group of friends were at school and at church, but my two younger sisters and my "unofficial" foster brother were my very best friends. My foster brother was a part of our family, even though my parents were never his legal guardians. The four of us kids were nearly bound at our hips.

My plan was to attend a four-year university as soon as I graduated. I was so ready for the life of adulthood and excited to take on a career that my family would be proud of. Since it was my senior year, I spent most of my time applying to the local colleges. As much fun as going to college far away sounded, I made the decision to stay nearby so that I would be close to my family and to Justin.

The fact that I was able to have my tuition paid at almost any California school due to my dad being a disabled vet had a great influence on my decision. My major would be in forensics, and at night I would finish what I had left of my modeling and acting classes which were more for fun than for a career.

Justin and I planned to attend the same college (if I was accepted into my top school) so we would be able to carpool and spend a lot of time together. With such big dreams, I was always looking for ways to spruce up my applications, which led to me trying out for the track team. I liked sports, and I really wanted to make myself look worthy of these amazing colleges. At that time, I had no idea the path I was about to tread on would lead to my downfall.

At my school, no one was ever cut from track tryouts, so I made the team, and everything was falling into place. My motive was stuck behind my plan for a successful future. Seeing as I absolutely hated running, I decided I needed to focus on a different part of track. My first thought was the hurdles, but that thought was squashed early on as I was barely five feet tall.

Then my coach brought me through some other events to

specialize in. I was too slow to get ahead of the packs during relay races; shot put and discus were completely out of the question; and my height deceived me yet again for the high jumps. Then my coach heard that I had a background in gymnastics and suggested I specialize in pole-vaulting.

As it turned out, I really enjoyed pole-vaulting, and I was good at it too! A few practices into the season, my pole-vaulting skills strengthened, and our team finally got to meet the real pole-vault coach. His name was Hans. He was standing in front of me, and I couldn't help but notice how good looking he was. In fact, we all noticed! I admit that I probably looked longer than I should have, but I couldn't help myself.

Hans introduced himself to us, and explained how his busy work schedule and volunteer hours at the fire department had prevented him from attending the first few practices, and he sincerely apologized for missing them. I was just happy he was here now. Not only was he good-looking, but he seemed sweet and attentive, and he seemed to know a lot about pole-vaulting, too.

After a few practices, I learned that Hans was almost four years older than me. He was also different than any of the other boys I knew at school, no doubt because of his age. And way different than my quiet, shy boyfriend. Justin who was athletic, blonde and blue eyed, and very polite.

Hans had a certain mystery about him that left me extremely confused. What was happening inside of me was different than I had known before. He was an experienced, tattooed, very outgoing man, with dark eyes, dark hair, and when he paid attention to me, it made me feel special. Nonetheless, I knew I had to put my head back in the game and shake off these thoughts and feelings, or I would end up in big trouble, so I tried... but I failed miserably.

In fact, my interest in Hans only grew throughout the season. So much so, that I started to let it affect my relationship with Justin and my parents. I constantly went to Hans for advice about boys and even advice on intimacy, thinking he wouldn't give me bad advice. We became closer throughout the practices and sports meets, and it didn't take long for me to become the focus of his attention, too.

Midway through the season, I sprained my ankle and couldn't participate as much in the practices in order to save myself for meets. This was when Hans asked me to help him demonstrate the drills and warm-ups while I healed. I didn't have to put much weight on my ankle, and my size would be helpful when he needed me to demonstrate the positioning.

Before I knew it, we were hanging out after practices, and meeting at his friend's house, and it wasn't always about pole-vaulting. I even caught myself getting jealous when he paid attention to the new girl vaulter who had joined the team midway through the season.

This one warm day at practice, Hans had taken off his shirt, and I noticed something dark on the back of his arm, so I asked him about it. He told me his friends had drawn on him with a permanent marker at his 21st birthday party the night before, and asked me sweetly, "Do you think you could help me clean it off? It's kind of hard for me to see it back there."

Of course, I jumped at the chance to lend a hand. Wanting desperately to fit in (but not being too obvious), I told him I would be happy to help.

I found a rag on the bench, and I slowly and carefully scrubbed on the markings until they were gone. Yet, it was in that moment that I realized I had feelings for him! I found myself daydreaming about a future together, and I was shocked. How could I be thinking this when Justin was still a big part of my life? Or was he? It was then that I knew I had to make a decision, because it wasn't fair to Justin. My heart was torn between two completely different personalities, which was all so new to me, and I wasn't sure what to do.

My whole life felt like it was spiraling out of control, and I didn't know how to fix it. I constantly started fights with my parents in regard to Hans and I being friends. In their wisdom they knew it was wrong and that Hans was playing me. They continued to warn me that he was dangerous and that he would take me down a path I never wanted to go. How could they know? They didn't understand how I felt and what we had, so why would I even listen? Maybe I took on a bit of my mother's stubbornness, but I was determined to prove them wrong.

My high school graduation was finally here, and in celebration, my parents threw me a huge pool party! Not only did many of my friends and family come to celebrate, but so did both Hans and Justin. What was I thinking? You could cut with a knife the tension in the air between Hans and everyone else at the party.

The day was spent swimming and playing different games that my mom had set up, although I hardly noticed. My eyes were focused only on Hans. I could see people starting to take notice and the whispers of it floating around like smoke.

When I was alone with a few of my closest friends, I showed off the rug burn I had on my back, like a badge of honor. I was proud of my rug-burned skin brought on by this handsome older man. Yet, I could see the worry in my friends' eyes as they too had thier doubts.

When the party was over and I said my good-byes, my parents once again reminded me how much they disliked him. "Why did you invite him, Amanda?" they asked. "We hoped to never see him again since you are out of school and no longer on the track team. What's going on?" Oh, if they only knew!

As a graduation gift, my Gran took me to Minnesota to spend

the week shopping, sightseeing, and getting away from all the drama that my graduation party had started. She and I were very close, so I felt comfortable sharing with her the emotional turmoil I was going through. When I was alone, I spent the time debating on whether I should stay with Justin or leave him for Hans.

Gran tried her best to distract me and help me to relax and enjoy our time together. We went to a live-action version of "The Birdcage," where she thought it would be hilarious not to tell me that the entire play was performed solely by men. We had a blast together, and the play was very funny and entertaining, but I couldn't kick aside my thoughts of the two guys in my life.

On our way back home, I made the decision to leave Justin. He wanted to graduate, get married, and have kids so much faster than I wanted. I was 17! I didn't want to even think about marriage and kids. I wanted to party and have fun, not settle down as a housewife. I wanted to live, and I knew that Hans could help me do that.

Shortly after I got back, I headed over to Justin's to break up with him. It made me sad, but I knew I had to. Justin immediately blamed Hans for everything, and the day ended with us going our separate ways.

I just knew that Hans was the one I wanted to be with, but deep down inside I was afraid to date him. I didn't understand why until years later. But at the time, it was a mystery.

I met up with Hans down the street from my house where we walked around and talked. With tears streaming down my face, I told him I wanted to be with him, but I was also afraid of not being with Justin. After all, Justin had been my first love and the only boy I had ever dated, kissed or been intimate with, and that he had a piece of my heart, and I wasn't sure if I could get it back. In my confusion, I told Hans how sorry I was, and that I changed my mind, and I wanted to go back to Justin.

Hans held me briefly, and then he said, "If you ever change your mind, Amanda, please let me know, because I feel like I am losing my only chance at true love." With that, Hans and I parted ways with the promise that we would still be friends.

The next day, I called Justin and explained my fears, and I was very grateful when he took me back. A few days later, he and his family went to Texas for their annual two-week visit. So I took this as an opportunity to see Hans as much as I could, but only as friends where we would watch movies and cuddle.

But things changed and sparks flew, and the cuddling turned into kissing and eventually into much more, with no thought of Justin at all. I soon realized that all I wanted was more and more of Hans, and I knew I had to end things with Justin... again.

A few weeks after Justin returned home, we quickly grew apart and we both realized we were going down different paths. I told him that right now all I wanted was to go to college and have fun like you're supposed to do, and he ended up breaking up with me.

The next day Hans asked me to be his girlfriend, which I gladly accepted. Things had moved so quickly for me; I had just left a three-year relationship, and here I was falling head-over-heels for someone else… in the blink of an eye.

I was thoroughly enjoying the honeymoon stage between Hans and me, and I was naïve to think that anything could ever ruin what we had. It was new. It was exciting.

Then one day he asked me if I was okay being in an open relationship. Apparently, this was the only way Hans could continue to be in a relationship with me. I thought it was a great idea! But only because I had no idea what this actually meant. I thought it was just being honest and open with another person, and with this man that was exactly what I wanted!

I found out later that my definition of an open relationship wasn't at all what Hans was expecting of me! What a surprise it was when I found out he wanted us to share the privacy of our bedroom and our bed with other couples.

2

Seventeen and Knew it All

I was seventeen and Hans was twenty-one, and I was so taken with this mature, experienced man who chose me, and I was eager to find out what it was like to be with someone new and exciting, and older too. I would constantly try different ways to see him. I have never done drugs, nor had I felt the need or desire to do them. It was Hans who was my drug of choice, and I was addicted.

What started out as holding hands and heavy kissing, quickly led to something more physical. I knew it was wrong and the voice in my head was screaming "NO!", but I did it anyway. This was when Hans started to manipulate me, showing me what made him happy and how much more he would "love" me if I listened and obeyed.

One night in particular stands out; after telling my parents I was working late, I stopped by Hans' friend's house. In the short time I was there, Hans told me he would really enjoy it if I helped him get off. Wanting to keep him happy, I agreed and got up to go to another room. But instead, he stayed on the couch and expected me to do it there in front of his friends, which I ended up doing.

I often had to push my guilt aside, as I felt great pleasure in the things we were doing because he knew so much more than I did, and I could tell how much he enjoyed it. For me, it was all about him and his approval of me.

His friends were also aware that I would do anything for him, and they thought I was the coolest girlfriend ever, being so open and obedient. I felt accomplished whenever he beckoned me. What girl wouldn't delight in seeing the man she loved being pleased by what they were doing? But in doing so, I also realized that I had lost what I could never get back. For I was so desperate to please him that I never noticed when my innocence was no longer part of who I was.

Though I was very happy being with Hans, no one I knew approved of our relationship. NO ONE! Some of my friends had even stopped talking to me and hanging out with me. This should have been a red flag, but I never noticed. Evidently, I tossed it away along with my innocence.

My parents, as well as other family members and close friends stayed by my side, but they were very blunt about their opinions. So vocal, in fact, that their disdain pushed me farther away from them and closer to Hans. They just didn't understand.

My friends tried to reason with me, suggesting that I leave him alone until after I turned eighteen to avoid any legal issues the age difference could cause, but I couldn't stay away from him. I was hooked.

The two of us would meet at the park or at his parents' house several times a week. My parents thought I was taking the dog on walks. This was the most harmless way I could see Hans. Anything else would cause a fight with my parents which I didn't want to deal with. Some people clearly knew what we were up to, but they didn't waste their breath discussing it with me, because they knew I wouldn't listen.

In fact, every time my guilt started to raise its ugly head and tried to move in and distract me, I purposely pushed it farther down inside until one day it was no longer a problem. Hans controlled my every thought, my every action, my every move, and, ever so slowly, I started to forget what my parents had taught me about God and His Son Jesus. I no longer wanted to hear it!

Hans told me I belonged to him now, and I believed him. Soon we found that spending time at his parents' house was always a good time, so we would go there often to swim and eat dinner with his family. It wasn't long before I started spending holidays at his house with his family instead of my own. I was on top of the world and completely mesmerized by this man who became my world, though I had no idea that soon my world would come crashing down.

Just when all the drama started to clear, we found ourselves in the middle of a statutory rape case against Hans. I guess we weren't as sneaky as we thought. Someone had called the school to report on our "inappropriate" relationship. For legal reasons, the school had to contact the authorities. Whoever made the call had to have come to the logical conclusion that Hans was my manipulative coach, and I was an underaged and easily influenced student. They just couldn't believe that we might actually be in love, which was what I believed myself for many years.

A few months later, the local authorities began a criminal investigation. The detective spoke with Hans's parents, some of the other athletes, and the head coach for their sides of the story. Fortunately, the head coach reported that he never thought our relationship was inappropriate. Hans and I were very cautious around the coach and other athletes on the school premises. We would barely even hold hands around our friends or families. It was only when we were alone that we would be riskier.

The detective finally spoke to my parents, and they had absolutely nothing good to say on the subject. In fact, they told the detective that if it were up to them, they would have Hans thrown in jail immediately.

It was a relief when a short time later the case was dropped because the authorities couldn't find any proof of statutory rape. Then I found out that the lead detective was a parent of one of

Hans's friends who didn't find our relationship to be worth the time and effort she would need to prove his guilt. Not to mention that I'd be turning eighteen in a few months.

Still, Hans wanted to play it safe, so he told me we had to stop everything that might cause him any more grief until I was of age. He was concerned about jeopardizing his future career in firefighting. I was so happy to see a hint of responsibility that I didn't even fight it.

Sadly, because of all this, what was once an unbreakable bond between myself, and my parents and siblings had now been shattered to pieces. I was constantly arguing with them, and I found myself staying out later and later, pushing every limit I could.

My once "good student" habits became very bad ones. My grades were slipping, and I often showed up to class very late or not at all. I don't know why I did it. I had never craved this sort of rebellion before. I hated going to school. It became such a waste of time and effort. I couldn't even pass the first year at the university.

Clearly, I was never going to graduate or get into the career I wanted. I didn't even have the motivation to fix my grades, so why should I stay in school? That was when I made the insane decision to let my full-ride scholarship to the university wither away with each negative grade percentage.

3

Almost an Adult

My 18th birthday was just a few days away. This was when the hell I would soon go through would ever so slowly begin it's destruction in me. Sinking deeper into darkness and losing any thought of who I used to be, I can barely admit this today, let alone put it on paper. But this was where it all began, when I willingly became Hans' real-life puppet.

Whatever Hans wanted me to do, I did. I was at the mercy of this insanely, strong emotion I thought was love. I so wanted it to be. Then at least there would be good reasons for my out-of-control conduct and rebellious actions. But sadly, I was too far away from the God I used to know, and at the mercy of Hans who soon became my god.

It started with Hans' friend, Tiffany, an aspiring playboy

model. At Hans' suggestion, she asked if I would be willing to assist her on an album cover that she was shooting. Me? On an album cover? Oh my gosh, I was so flattered. I had always wanted to model and had actually been taking modeling classes for a while. Not to mention this was going to be published on an actual album for everyone to see! It filled me with great excitement, and pumped my ego until I was giddy at the thought of being in the pictures.

The photo shoot was set up for later that week, which was the week of Thanksgiving. My parents and sisters had gone to visit our family in another state. I couldn't join them because of work, so I stayed with my aunt.

On the day of the shoot, I told my aunt I was going to hang out with some friends, and that I'd be back later that night. I didn't want her to know that friend happened to live with Hans. Tiffany's boyfriend lived there too.

When I got to Hans' house, Tiffany's friend did my hair. I even got to go shopping in her closet to see what outfit would work best for the album cover design. They dressed me up in these pretty lace boy shorts and a tank top. I looked very young, but evidently that was the look they wanted. I barely even recognized myself. Once we were all fixed up, we went to Tiffany's mom's house to utilize the back drops.

The first poses were taken in the master bedroom. Then we migrated into a bubble bath scene. In these shots, I was merely Tiffany's assistant, making sure her hair was out of her face and the lighting was right. But then it was my turn to join her. The two of us were back in the bedroom on top of the bed, with a fur blanket underneath us. I sat with my bare back to the camera and wearing my lacy shorts.

It was so subtle, but in my heart I knew this was not how I was raised. Yet, Satan had a hold of me, and he would not let go... nor did I want him to. I was on my way to stardom of the worse kind, and I no longer cared that I was getting lost in this heavy blanket of sin.

Tiffany's arms were wrapped around my back and her face was resting on my shoulders. My face never showed, only hers. Not only did this add some mystic to the images, but for now I wanted to keep my identity safe.

My parents would have never approved of the nature of these images, and I knew I would be in mounds of trouble even though I knew I would be 18 years old before anyone saw these pictures. I would still suffer their wrath.

When we finished, I went back to my aunt's house and told her I would be spending the night at another girlfriend's house for a small party she was throwing. My trusting aunt obviously didn't realize I'd be meeting Hans at said girlfriend's house because that was so unlike what I would do. I spent the night there and went to work the next day without any doubt in my mind that there would be no repercussions from the previous day.

The next day, Tiffany emailed me the pictures from the photo shoot which I deleted immediately, but my parents ended up seeing them later. Needless to say, they flipped out as any parent would.

As I was getting in my car after work, Hans' mom called me and told me it wasn't safe for me to go home and that I should come to her house instead. She was clearly in a panic, and I still had no idea what was going on. Then I heard the yelling. My parents had shown up at Hans' to confront him and his roommate.

I went straight home, as I wasn't about to avoid my own family. As soon as I walked inside, I saw my parents and siblings and my close friends sitting in the living room. Was this an intervention? They all told me how afraid they were for my future. They blamed Hans and Tiffany saying the pictures that they had talked me into posing for were going to take me down a path of pornography and depression. They even cast blame on my poor, innocent aunt, who had no idea what I had done since I lied about where I was going. I thought my lies would protect her just in case this happened, but I was so very wrong.

It was indeed an intervention, a very unnecessary intervention, which at the time I fully believed. They all were completely overreacting, and I told them so. Sadly, their intervention did exactly the opposite of what they intended. I felt more pushed away than ever, and I gladly welcomed Hans and his family's comfort in return.

More so than ever, I was finding excuses to be with Hans' family and stayed as far away from my own home as possible. My 18th birthday was spent with Hans at the tattoo parlor where I got several piercing, knowing that my parents would not approve, but I no longer cared. But at last, I was 18 years old, and no one could tell me what to do or how to do it. I was a full-grown adult who could make her own decisions!

A few days after my birthday, my mom and dad sat me down at the kitchen table in another attempt to "get through" to me. Again, they told me how this path was going to lead to one I would eventually regret. Once again, I ignored them. They didn't know what they were talking about. Hans would never let anything bad happen to me. He loved me and I loved him. So, I ignored their warnings and advice and started looking into moving in with Hans after the new year.

My life wasn't going exactly as I had hoped, but with Hans by my side, I knew I would be just fine.

4

New Year - New World

It was New Year's Eve 2006, and Hans invited me to a party at his older stepbrother Cory's house. Even though I was freshly 18, I still lived under my parents' roof, so I still had to ask their permission to go. I knew this wasn't going to be an easy task since my relationship with them had only worsened.

Not only had I stopped following their advice, but I stopped living by their rules. Hans even bought me a secondary cell phone so they couldn't try to control that aspect of our ability to communicate. That said, I knew if I went to this party without their permission, it would only make things worse. My parents didn't trust Hans or Cory at all. I didn't know Cory very well, so I couldn't even offer the words to make them more comfortable about allowing me to go.

After a very long discussion and a lot of pleading, my parents finally gave in and said I could go. Though they did have their stipulations for me to be home at a decent time, check in upon arrival, and check in upon leaving. They even tried to throw in Hans attending church with us for just one service. Hans declined quickly though, due to him being an Atheist, but I was still allowed to go to the party.

This was the first opportunity for me to attend a real house party! In Hans' world, my reputation was slowly meeting everyone's approval. It meant a lot to me because it meant a lot to Hans. Regardless of this new lifestyle, I was careful to only drink non-alcoholic beverages. The last thing I needed was to come home drunk and face the wrath of my parents. Again!

On the way to the party, Hans was telling me story after story about how cool Cory and his wife were. Apparently, they were known to throw the best parties around. My heart was trembling with anticipation. I wanted so much for Hans to think of me as cool!

When we arrived, Cory's wife, Destiny, came over and introduced herself. She was stunning, and her confidence radiated with every breath she took. She had this blatant happiness about her that gleamed through her smile. Destiny welcomed us and then ran upstairs to change before the rest of their guests arrived.

When she came back downstairs, I could not take my eyes off of her as her outfit was incredibly revealing. You could see each and every curve, for it was purposely designed to show off everything. I shuddered at the thought of myself in that outfit. I would have been so uncomfortable and even somewhat embarrassed.

As more people arrived, I was shocked and awed at the skimpy outfits everyone had on, including the men! Suddenly I felt very overdressed. Unbeknownst to me this party was a lingerie theme party. Everyone was standing around mingling, drinking, and snacking. This was when I concluded that this was the coolest party ever.

I began day-dreaming that this party was going to be like those parties you see in the movies. Champagne, kissing at midnight, and dancing with your crush. But then things started to get very weird and very loose. I couldn't believe my eyes.

I asked Hans if their parties were always like this. "Of course, they are. Destiny's a porn star," he replied. Everything made sense after that. I had never known anyone to have or desire a career in porn, and I had no idea how to feel.

Before long the girls started entertaining the crowd, and Hans pushed me in closer to join them. I was appalled, feeling very out of place and on display. As the night became more wild, it was clear to Hans that I wanted to leave. We said our good-byes and they told me how cute and fun they thought I was, and that I was welcome back whenever I wanted.

On the way home, Hans asked me what I thought of the party.

"Interesting," was the only word I could think of. It was a new experience for me, and I told him I wasn't really sure how to feel. I was still taken aback by everything I had witnessed. My life was very PG-13, to say the least, and I definitely wasn't ready to watch the freakish antics of all those people doing what they were doing to each other. I was shell-shocked. Maybe I would have felt differently had I been drinking. But I'm thankful that I wasn't.

Before I fell asleep, I decided that this evening would remain my little secret. No one else needed to know. Besides, how could I ever begin to explain what I saw, when I wasn't even sure myself!

As I look back on all of this today, I can't begin to fathom that this was the lifestyle I truly believed I wanted to live. That I had to live, and at any cost!

Soon, I found myself craving it, and I could not stop until I had it all!

5

On My Own... Sort Of

By the end of January, things reached their boiling point with my parents, and I moved in with Hans and his friends Mark and Tina, who Hans had known from high school. They had an extra bedroom they wanted to rent out so they could save for their wedding, and they offered it to us. Within a matter of days, Hans and I moved into the fully furnished two-bedroom, two-bathroom apartment. I was over the moon with joy.

Mark was a great roommate, but it seemed the wedding stress started to take its toll on Tina. Since my only job at the time was trying to find a job, I offered to help Tina make all of the favors for her wedding to which she was very grateful.

Before I knew it, Valentine's Day was upon us, and I had spent last bit of savings on a card and some chocolates. Hans was the one working full-time and his gift to me reflected that. He had given me a gorgeous ruby and diamond necklace and an expensive cheetah print duvet cover I had been eyeing. I felt spoiled like a princess.

Everything seemed to be falling into place until Hans told me that he needed help paying the bills. Feeling somewhat guilty, I started looking harder for a job. As I searched the ads, I jokingly mentioned to Hans one day about doing something crazy like in the movie "Coyote Ugly." (This movie was all about sexy girls tending bar to a very rowdy crowd. As the night progressed, the girls would climb on top of the bar and dance together, and the crowd would go wild.) I was kidding, of course, because I was still too young to bartend. However, it seemed to have given Hans an idea. Or maybe this was his plan all along.

Without the least hesitation, Hans looked at me and said, "Maybe you should try out for amateur night at the local strip club. You're old enough and I know those girls make a boat load of money! And you're a great dancer, too."

I was shocked by his suggestion. Amateur night? Me? Naked in front of a bunch of strangers throwing money at me? My confidence level shrunk at the thought. I had never even been inside of a strip club, so how could I ever be a dancer? Then realizing how short we were on money, and with Hans pleading with me, I decided, "Why not?"

I went to the club and attempted to do what was expected of me, and it went about as horrible as you would expect. This was when my determination kicked in. Embarrassed by my performance, I desperately wanted to show Hans my worth. I needed him to be proud of me. I wanted him to know that I was as cool as Destiny. Now more than ever, I was determined to win the contest!

Destiny heard about my failed tryout, and she came down the next week to show me some basic moves that she had learned while dancing. I definitely didn't want to embarrass myself again, nor Hans either. She even came to the club to cheer me on and ease my nerves.

It was my night to shine, and this time I took first place and was offered a full-time job as a dancer! My ego was pumped, and Hans was so proud of me! He went on and on about the fun I was going to have and how much money I was going to make for us.

I accepted the job offer that same night with nightmare thoughts of my family in the back of my mind. They would be crushed if they ever found out. But since we hardly ever talked anymore, I figured there was no way they'd ever know.

The next week the four of us went shopping. Hans and Cory even picked my stage name: Madison. Hans thought I'd make even more money if I played up the fact that I was young, so he cut up some jean shorts and skirts for me to wear on stage.

Hans's friends were also excited about my new career. They told Hans how cool he was for letting me do it. But it was never really my choice. It was what Hans wanted for me. And Hans always got what he wanted.

On the other hand, Tina was absolutely appalled that I was willing to be a stripper and immediately began treating me differently. She told me stripping was gross and that she would never let Mark talk her into doing that kind of work, no matter how desperate for money they were.

I attempted to shake off her bullying comments, but they stuck with me long after she said them because deep down I knew she was right. I had no business in that business, but Hans wanted it for me, and so I did it for him. This began a pattern of what our lives became over the next several years. Whatever Hans wanted Hans got! No matter what! Little did I know that "I was being programed to say Yes!"

After Mark and Tina returned from their honeymoon, Tina didn't like the idea of us living with them anymore. She started leaving notes around the apartment telling us not to touch things; the washer, the dryer, the thermostat, and "her" diet sodas. She even taped the thermostat so no one but her was able to change the temperature. The apartment began to feel extremely claustrophobic.

By this time, I had been dancing a few months, and we were able to build a decent savings account. We decided to put that money towards a new place to live with all the furnishings. We told Mark we were moving, and he understood, with no hard feelings.

This would be the third time we had moved since I moved out of my parents' place. I so wanted this two-bedroom, two-bath apartment to be stable enough to provide a bit of longevity, especially since we signed a one-year lease. But only time would tell.

The new place was nice enough, and it had a lot more room than any other place we had lived, but unfortunately it wasn't in the greatest neighborhood. Fortunately, it was closer to the club, but it was too far for Hans to continue volunteering, so he had to quit the fire department, though he didn't seem too upset about it.

Hans took a part-time job, but it didn't last long when he was injured and had to quit. I was grateful to be dancing full-time as we were relying solely on my income from the club while Hans tried to get on with a new fire department. He took his EMT certification test twice, and twice he failed!

On top of that, California had put a three-year hiring freeze on firefighters and paramedics, so Hans decided to take a break in hopes that he could study for future testing. At least, that's what he told me, though I was never able to verify, nor had I ever thought to.

I had made several new friends at the club, and Hans and I started hosting our own parties. Being a stripper brought in the money we needed to do the things we wanted.

How foolish can one be when they're far too young and have no idea what the world is all about? Unfortunately, I learned too late.

6

~~~

New Puppy/Newer Adventures

In August 2007, Hans received a phone call from his friend, Matt, who told him that he had found two puppies, and Matt thought we might be able to help him find a home for them. We went to see the puppies, and I fell in love immediately. I asked Hans if we could please keep the one with cropped ears, and he said, "Yes!" I was over the moon thrilled with our new family member. We immediately went to the pet store and bought everything she could possibly want and need.

Life was good and our "family" had grown because now we had our sweet Lucy. It felt like we were finally building something that just might last. I was so happy. These bursts of happiness were no doubt what kept me believing that this was where I was supposed to be.

The club had their photographer take pictures of me for the inside advertising. Since it was free, Hans suggested we get "family" pictures with Lucy. They started with the three of us sitting together and ended up with both me and Hans shirtless, and me kneeling and looking up at him while he smiled at the camera.

Toward the end of September, Hans started to drop hints about how I should follow in Destiny's footsteps and start doing movies in Los Angeles.

"Think of the money you could make for us! And you could choose whoever you wanted to film with," Hans boasted proudly one afternoon. But his proposed idea left me extremely uncomfortable.

We both knew that this could cause a huge rift between not only us, but with my parents, too. I wasn't sure why I should even care what they thought at this point. I was barely on speaking terms with them, all because I had chosen Hans instead of them.

I wasn't aware of it at first, but it always seemed to be about the money with Hans. And because money was so important to him, it became important to me. I didn't want him to worry about our finances, so I started asking some of the other dancers who came through the club what it was like to be in "those" movies.

When these dancers learned that Destiny was my sister-in-law, they started telling me all the juicy details, and I'll admit I was intrigued.

I was desperate to have the confidence and popularity of these film stars, and to be as sexy as these girls were, all while making a whole bunch of money. The money was, of course, the most important thing, so why not give it a try? What could it hurt? I was already a stripper. How much worse could it be in the movies?

Hans had planted the seed, and I really had nothing to lose. Certainly not my family! They were already gone. So the decision was made, and I was going to give it a try... no matter the costs or the consequences.

Once I made this decision to enter into the darkness of perversion where anything goes, there was no going back to the girl I used to be. Was that only a year ago? Oh dear God, what have I done?

Looking back, I realize the pain my family must have felt as they sadly watched what I had become. To this day, I don't know what I was thinking. I loved my mom and dad and my family so much, and I never intended to hurt them.

The only person I was thinking about at the time was Hans, and Hans was only thinking about the money I could make for him! And because I was so focused on making him proud, I started to forget about the person I had been before: The one with morals and values. The one who was proud of her accomplishments and the woman she had high hopes of becoming one day.

Yet the memory of all that seemed to be too far in the rearview, and getting farther and farther away with every choice I continued to make.

7

Lights - Camera - Action!

With my bags packed, I was off to spend a few days in the life of an X-rated movie star. Hans and I headed to Cory's for another one of their parties, but this time we would be spending the night so that Destiny and I could head to Los Angeles the next morning.

Unlike the last party, this time I knew what I was getting myself into when I went to their cops and robbers theme party. This party was similar to the other one, with lots of scantly clothed guests, and the drinks were flowing. However, unlike last time, I joined the others when they all started drinking, which made me feel more at ease. My confidence level had grown so much since I had been here last. Plus, this time I was quite intoxicated and had no inhibitions whatsoever!

Though the evening was unclear, I was pretty certain that I had made the night memorable for someone, although I had no idea who until the next morning when I heard Cory and Hans talking. My memory was blurry, but evidently I had done what I was told, and Hans was proud of me again. Wasn't that the goal? Cory winked at me when he saw me come into the kitchen. All I could do was smile back, for at that moment I had a feeling he and Hans had convinced me to do something I probably wouldn't have done sober.

Whatever happened, it wasn't my first time, and it was quite certain not to be my last. I would also bet that whatever I did was Hans idea, and me being his obedient puppet, I jump at yet another chance to please him. However, this time I was glad I was intoxicated. It helped me get through it, and to forget it, too!

As soon as the car was packed, Destiny and I headed down to LA without mentioning anything about the night before. It was like it never happened.

I was so nervous the morning of the first scene. I had no idea what to expect. Destiny told me I didn't have to go through with it if I didn't want to. But I wanted to at least try. Hans would be so disappointed if I didn't. She reassured me it was only for her website, so if I changed my mind during the scene, it would be fine.

The first scene fell apart very quickly, and I thought my movie days were over before they had ever started. I told Hans about the painful and disastrous scene, and he decided that maybe I should go into this new filming career gradually until I knew what I was doing.

The next day I contacted an agency in LA that Destiny had recommended, and I signed a contract with them stating that I would only perform specific things with certain people until further notice.

Everything had happened so quickly. This was when I realized that in a little over a year after moving out of my parents' house, I was officially in the film industry! I went from a career-driven high school student, to starring in my own Triple X rated movies. Oh how proud my parents would be! But I didn't feel the least bit remorseful. I had been programed to say "Yes", and I kept saying "Yes" to everything I was given, to every opened door no matter what was behind it.

With every passing day, I felt less and less shame, until one day I felt nothing at all. No guilt, no regret. No nothing!

8

Embracing the New Me

I was dancing at the club part-time and also part-time commuting to LA for days or sometimes weeks in order to shoot the scenes they had set up for me. Often times I would find myself getting caught up in the lights and cameras, and it made me feel as if I were an actual star. "Oh the tangled web we weave when first we practice to deceive." And I was drowning in it.

A short time later, I decided it was best for me to quit dancing. This gave me more time and opportunity to do the things I needed to do, like filming, which was a lot more lucrative. But still I wanted more exposure.

I stayed with one of the girls who was in the business, and

she introduced me to her friend Tony. He was a publicist in the industry and wanted to help get my name out there.

Tony took me to parties, clubs, and red-carpet events where he introduced me to all the right people. I felt special whenever I walked into an event and was given instant VIP status. My name was getting more known, and I was moving up quickly. Fame was what it was all about in this business! No matter how it was achieved! Or so I thought at the time.

It all happened so fast. Soon, I was co-hosting with Tony on his internet radio show. My agent and Tony had talked to several companies, and shortly after, I was offered my first high rate of pay for my film work, mostly because it would be the first scene involving full sex.

While the contracts were being signed, Tony called and told me that he was asked to host the Miss Nude Canada Pageant, and invited me to go with him. Though I had no idea what this event was, it sounded interesting and, of course, I said yes! It would also be something I could put on my resumé.

I was due to shoot my new scene after I returned home from Canada. Before I left I had to schedule my monthly STI check in order to be available to shoot the scene. I was due for mine, so I decided to test early to make sure all was good.

I was waiting to board the plane when I received a call from the industry doctor telling me I had tested positive for Gonorrhea.

Had I been in any other profession, I would have freaked out, but it was pretty common to have this in the industry I was in. I explained to the doctor about going to Canada, and he said I'd be fine to wait a week on the medicine, but not to be intimate with anyone while I was gone. Since my plans only included co-hosting this pageant and nothing else, I knew it wouldn't be a problem.

On the night of the pageant, we got all dressed up and headed down to the local strip club. I had no idea what to expect at the club, but we were treated like VIPs from the moment we walked in.

I had seen girls dance before, but nothing like these girls! They climbed all the way up into the rafters in the ceiling and performed for the crowd. One girl even brought out this gigantic champagne glass filled with bubbles and performed her whole routine in the glass. It was very impressive.

The final two days were filled with shooting music videos for one of Canada's premiere rock bands. It was interesting to see what goes into the making of music videos. Not only did we get to watch them plan the videos, but we were invited to be the girls in the videos as well. I doubt many people in the States had heard of the band because they were from Canada, but I was pleased that I could put another item on my industry resumé that not many others could.

I left a day before the others so I could start the medicine in time to shoot the scene that had been scheduled. The doctor gave me the pills, and he also gave me some for Hans just to be cautious. Within an hour, I had a reaction to the medicine and thought I was going to die. The medicine was meant to clear out your entire system within twenty-four hours so you can only imagine the agony. I hoped that this first time was also the last time I would ever have to go through it, and thank God it was.

We had rescheduled my big debut scene for a few weeks just to be on the safe side. But because of the Adult Video News (AVN) Convention (where people would come to meet the stars and see them receive awards), we ended up not being able to shoot the scene until February. This would not only be my first big public "outing" in the United States as Madison, but also my first time to Las Vegas.

Thanks to all the publicity Tony had helped with, I was asked to be one of the trophy girls for the award show! Not only would this give me more exposure in the industry, but it would also be the first ever show broadcast on HBO. It all made me feel so important. I felt needed and, as always, it had very much pleased Hans, which made my life so much easier.

The day of the show I went to the rehearsal and was able to meet all the "big stars" of the industry that were also going to be in the show. After a few hours of figuring out all the details, we were excused to get dressed for the actual show. I threw on the only formal dress I had with me. Then I put on my makeup and did my hair to the best of my ability, and met up with Hans to go back to the event.

The show went amazingly, and I was able to attend the after parties as well. It really was such a surreal experience. At the after party, not only where the big names in my industry there, but also UFC fighters who I was able to mingle with, which made me feel like I was someone important. I mean, how many times do you get a chance to hang out with famous celebrities on a one-on-one basis?

My next major money-making event was going to be during Super Bowl weekend that year. For several years Destiny had hosted a party where she would bring in a few girls from the sex industry as entertainment, and she invited me to be one of them. All the guys who attended this party purchased tickets in advance, and they were all well aware that they also needed to bring a lot of cash with them for their "entertainment".

There were booths set up in the back rooms during the game so that each girl had an area to dance and perform privately for their paying customers. Then the four of us would perform a live action show in front of the whole crowd during half-time, while an insane amount of cash was tossed out to us. Once the show was over, we changed and went back to our booths to dance privately until the game was over.

Although these girls had been in this industry for several years and had done many more scenes than I had done, by night's end, I was feeling every bit as famous and loved. I was finally getting a taste of what being a big-name actress would be like, not to mention that I made over two thousand dollars in just a matter of hours! This was enough money to hold us over until I had my "big film scene" in just a few weeks. Hans would be very pleased.

Unfortunately, the deeper I fell into this demonic trap of darkness, the less and less it affected my conscience, which by this time was almost nonexistent. I had nearly forgotten who I was and had become obsessed with fame, money and keeping Hans happy. The morals and beliefs I was brought up with had been completely tossed aside.

9

My Big Debut

The time had finally come for me to shoot my very first full sex scene. My agents reassured me that everything was going to be fine and if things went wrong, or I started to feel uncomfortable, I could call them and they would fix whatever the problem was.

Hans drove me to the location since he had come to Los Angeles with me because he knew how nervous I was; it was, after all, my biggest scene yet.

When I arrived on the set, there was a makeup artist waiting for me to help things go easier, and that I would have the exact look they were going for. It was nice not having to stress over my appearance since the makeup artist would be there the whole time to help me look my best, just like in the real Hollywood movies!

I was introduced to Ethan, the male talent I would be working with, and, to my surprise, he seemed just as nervous about the scene as I was. He tried to calm my nerves to make this as easy as possible on both of us.

We started the shoot with pictures of just me looking cute and innocent, and then slowly worked into sexier poses. It was at this point that Ethan joined me in the photos and the video camera started rolling.

I rather not go into details of what took place after this, because this is not the person I am anymore. But I'm sure, with any sort of imagination, you can picture what took place when the cameras began to roll, and nothing was held back by either of us.

The next day, Hans and I drove home, and I was able to spend a few days relaxing. The company that shot the scene told my agency I had done a spectacular job, so we decided it was time to add these scenes to the list of what companies could book me for when I was in town.

Because I didn't want to get overbooked, I set a high rate for those scenes and also set a maximum amount of them I would do per month. I didn't want to end up being over shot and ruin the longevity of my career. My agent agreed with these stipulations, and we began booking scenes for the next few trips to Los Angeles.

For the next several months, I spent half my time living and working in LA, and the rest in Sacramento. Most nights were spent making appearances at parties, red carpet events and just making sure I kept my name in the limelight so my fans would not forget me, or that I would not fade into another drop-out starlet. It was Hans' greatest fear that one day no one would remember my name.

By this time, I had moved in with one of my girlfriends in LA. Hans would come down every few trips so that I was able to see him, and we could spend time together when I wasn't filming. Besides, he wasn't working so there was no reason for him to stay home.

Whenever we'd go out, Hans would make sure that my hair, makeup, and outfit always looked perfect, because, as he always told me, "Even at home, you have to worry about your appearance." It was like living in a glass house.

No matter what mood I was in, I was always supposed to be at my best and look my best for my public, even when my public was nowhere to be seen! Even when my public was only Hans!

It was all part of this life I had chosen to live, and I often wondered how long it would be before I would tire of it all. I had completely forgotten that it was what was on the inside that mattered.

10

Making a Name in a Fallen World

One night, I left late to drive to LA for an early morning scene and found myself thinking how much easier it would be if I just lived in LA.

That afternoon, I noticed a red bump that was starting to hurt on my thigh. Thinking it was an ingrown hair, I tried to pop it, but it only got worse. My roommate told me to get to the hospital because it looked like I had gotten a staph infection from the scene. After calling Hans, he told me to drive back to Sacramento, and he would take me.

By the time I got there, I felt awful and just wanted my mom. Even though I barely talked to her anymore, I called her. She told me I was being overly dramatic and was probably fine.

I did end up popping and draining the now massive bump and going to urgent care. They confirmed it was staph and gave me antibiotics and sent me on my way.

The next four months was just routine, me working in Los Angeles and then coming back to Sacramento. I was getting tired of always being on the go and trying to jam everything I needed or wanted to do into two weeks in each city. It made much more sense if we just moved to Los Angeles and me not have to commute, since I was the only one working. But first I had to get permission from Hans.

We talked that night, and after much debate, it was decided that us moving to LA was best. However, once the decision was made, it was time for me to come clean to my parents about my profession. Though I dreaded so much telling them because I knew they would never understand. What parent would? But still they needed to know.

However, before I was able to tell them myself, an old acquaintance from high school had already taken it upon herself to email them. She told them everything, and she even attached one of the DVDs with me on the front cover. I can only imagine their shock and horror as well as their pain.

Before we left for LA, Hans and I stopped by his parents for a tearful goodbye, and then we headed over to say goodbye to my family. It crushed my heart to see them so broken and emotional. Not that I blamed them. I knew it was because they loved me and that they were seriously concerned for my well-being. They didn't want me to go, but nothing they could say would change my mind. The decision had already been made.

As we were leaving their house, my dad, foster brother, and my sister's boyfriend cornered Hans in the backyard, and they had a serious talk with him while I was in the house with my mom who couldn't stop crying.

The last thing she said to me before I left was, "I love you, Amanda, and I pray to God that our Christmas won't be spent identifying the body of our eldest daughter who had been raped and left dead in a gutter." I was speechless. Those were some of the harshest words my mother had ever said to me, even to this day.

I cried all the way to LA, while Hans angrily told me some of what the boys had said to him.

"How can you say you love her and then allow other men to do this stuff to her?" they yelled, not caring if anyone heard. "What kind of a monster are you anyway? Have you no heart or no feelings at all?" Their scolding was every bit as harsh as my mom's, and in our own personal silence, we digested every word as we drove to our new LA home.

After we were moved in and settled, my days were spent working on the set, where not only did I star in the scenes, but I was also doing hair and makeup for other actresses. I would also make several appearances at parties, red carpet events and movie premiers, or I'd be at the gym working with my personal trainer. It was important for me to get all the exposure I could, and crucial for me to stay in shape.

Hans would accompany me to some of the special events and, if he went, he wanted to be on the red-carpet walking with me and not just off to the side holding my purse. Most of the events I attended were for red carpet pictures, but I was only allowed inside for a few minutes because I was not yet twenty-one.

The two biggest events we attended were a large feature film premier and a Halloween party hosted by a clothing designer. At the premiere, Hans walked the red carpet with me along with a friend of mine who was a veteran of the industry. Then the three of us continued inside to watch the film on the big screen with close to a hundred other people.

I never imagined I'd be invited to these big events since I was still fairly new to the industry. But because of how I ran my bookings, I was able to be selective and work with some of the biggest name companies.

This same friend invited us to join her at the Halloween party in Hollywood, where we hung out with several famous rock stars and other clothing designers. The party was large enough to have the LAPD as security, and they kept a helicopter flying over the area the entire night. After we parked our cars, we were all shuttled up to the house because it was such an exclusive event.

Shortly after these events, my agent informed me that I was

not to have any more piercing or tattoos, not to gain any weight or change the color of my hair, because one of the larger companies had approached him with talk of a contract for me to sign, and I would work exclusively with them.

This was exciting news since I wanted so badly to be one of those big stars who made a ton of money and had lots of fans, and to be considered one of the more elite girls in the industry, even though the industry was porn. The longer I did these films, the more I realized just how many dedicated fans these films brought in. The numbers were staggering.

I felt grateful that I had finally made a name for myself. Not only was I shooting scenes for small internet companies, but I was able to socialize with some of the biggest named stars, and they knew who I was! This had always been my goal.

I was being noticed and becoming even more famous, and I was on top of the world. Little did I know at the time that what goes up, must come down. My head was so far up in the clouds that I knew if I ever fell, I would fall hard, and it would be excruciating.

During a challenging period in my life, I had come to the realization that I was in a relationship with someone who had an habitual controlling nature. Hans had certain expectations of me that were difficult to meet, and he was so controlling that I struggled to maintain my own sense of self.

In order to keep some of our bedroom activities special, Hans suggested I let him become a dominant partner since I would not do those kinds of scenes.

He first began by setting rules for me to follow, some of which were relatively easy though a bit strange, such as addressing him as 'Sir', and to always capitalize words referring to him whenever I sent him a text. He expected me to not wear much clothing when at home, and to sit at his feet as if my presence was below him. He also picked out what I would wear every day, and expected my hair and makeup to always be done.

As the months passed, the punishments for not obeying them were much more severe and often very cruel, leaving me with cuts and bruises. He expected me to be completely submissive, even when it came to basic daily activities.

Over time, it became quite clear that the relationship had become extremely unhealthy with Hans exerting a significant amount of control over my life.

I was unsure how to stop what he had started, but I knew if I didn't do something soon, it was not going to turn out well for me at all. This was when I decided it was time to leave LA, and see if going back to Sacramento would bring things down. Plus Hans missed his family and friends, so we were still commuting back and forth anyways. He told me he felt isolated and alone living in LA since everything was always about "Madison".

11

My Mother Was Right

After the AVN Convention, we would be moving back to Sacramento. I attended the convention as a makeup artist this time, but I still attended some parties. I was nominated for an award at one of the smaller award shows, but sense I wasn't 21, I couldn't get into the venue and even though we asked, Hans could not accept my award for me. God really had His hand in that one, because years later it would come out that was a blessing in disguise.

So, we moved back to Sacramento, and instead of getting a hotel room each trip to LA, I made arrangements with Lily, who was also in films, to stay at her house with her and her husband,

Jayden who was also in the sex industry. This worked out well for us, and she and I became close friends. It was nice to be able to just be my real self at their house.

Lily and I spent our days off shopping and working out together or going out to eat. In one of our conversation, Lily shared with me, "In between my films, I started making monthly trips to Carson City, Nevada, to work at the Bunny Ranch Brothel in order to bring in more money." Then she suggested that I look into this, to help bring in some extra money for us, too.

It sounded great, but unfortunately working in Carson might be too risky for me, since I had several family members who lived in the vicinity. I didn't want them to see me driving around town or inquiring about why I was there. So, for the time being, I continued to work with my agency.

Since money was starting to get tight, and I wasn't willing to risk being in Carson, Hans suggested I do "privates" (basically inter-industry escorting). A director friend of mine, Gavin, helped me find clients and he booked appointments for me. He never took any money from me so, in my naivety, I didn't see him as the pimp he was.

After I had finished filming for a few weeks, I stopped by Lily's to check on her. That was when she informed me she had talked to the owner of the Ranch, and he offered me a job. Not only was the money a lot better, but it was a more controlled environment, since Lily hated the idea of me doing privates.

Gavin text me letting me know he had an appointment for me at his back house that night. Lily asked me to check in with her before and after because she had a bad feeling. I let her know I was still waiting for the client when Gavin walked in. I decided to get dressed and head home when he asked me to come talk and started to get handsy.

Before I knew it, Lily's suspicions had been confirmed, and long story short, Gavin had sexually assaulted me. He said I had owed it to him for him booking me appointments. I forgot to tell Lily I had left his house because I was so upset, and she called me freaking out.

When I got home, she met me outside and tried to console me. I decided to leave LA early, and that I would report him. Even though I had handprint bruises, a confirmed doctor's note saying it was visible that I was assaulted, $1000 cash attached to any apology note from Gavin, the district attorney told me she wouldn't press charges because no jury would believe a port star could be raped.

I wanted to get out of LA, and I was more than willing to entertain the idea of the Bunny Ranch now. So, Lily and I talked about it for a while, and I asked as many questions as I could so that I could share them with Hans when we talked. Once Hans learned the money was better, he was definitely onboard for me to check it out.

In mid-May, Hans and I traveled to Carson City to meet Lily and the owner of the Ranch for a sit-down discussion about a new job opportunity. During the meeting, the owner patiently answered all our questions, provided a tour of the facilities, and explained the potential income compared to working in films. Wow was I surprised by how much more I could make.

Grateful for the insights, we had a follow-up lunch with Lily to delve deeper into our decision-making process. Ultimately, we agreed that this opportunity was worth considering, even if it meant leaving the film industry behind.

I made a call to the Ranch and scheduled my first two-week trip for the end of June. My plan was to continue working part-time in films during this trial period. However, if my experience at the Ranch proved to be worthwhile, I was prepared to quit my film career.

Because of the assault, I was still haunted by nightmares and panic attacks. I also struggled with intimacy, both physical and emotional, especially with Hans. My apprehensions about how I would manage at the Ranch, where intimacy was a key component of the job, loomed large.

I had regressed to allowing Hans to take control in the bedroom to help me cope. What had begun as playful restraints and mild BDSM had evolved into something way more intense. The more he learned about using the chains and ropes, the worse it became.

I often had to sleep at the bottom of the bed or on the floor. I wasn't allowed to make eye contact with him unless he said it was okay. He always ate first as I sat at his feet, then I was allowed to eat on the floor. I was never allowed to tell him "No" to any sexual activities. I was also to crawl around the house and not walk, always fully made up with my hair done.

However, as time went on, the rules became even more restrictive, and I found myself facing consequences for not adhering to them, like sleeping without clothes or a blanket, and being locked in the dogs' kennel or in a dark closet or sleeping with the dogs and taking only cold showers. It was brutal.

As my departure to Carson City approached, I packed my bags, bid farewell to Hans and our dogs, and embarked on my two-week journey.

Upon arriving, I went straight to the doctor for a mandatory medical screening. Once I was cleared, I could start booking appointments. Following the medical checkup, I attended a house meeting with the other girls. These meetings served to introduce me to the team, set weekly goals and competitions, update us on Ranch news and publicity efforts, and end on a positive note, with each of us sharing something uplifting.

Next, Lily familiarized me with the house rules and policies, initiating my training. We spent several hours going over procedures, customer negotiations, and acquiring necessary supplies while meeting the staff.

About halfway through Lily's twelve-hour shift, we began actively working, participating in "line ups." Line ups occurred when the front bell signaled a customer's arrival. All the girls on shift would assemble by the front door, introducing themselves, and the customer would choose a girl for a tour.

If chosen, the girl would guide the customer through the facility and conclude the tour in her room for further discussions and negotiations. Those girls who were not selected were expected to remain in the front parlor or bar area until they booked a session with a customer. Once a session was booked, others could resume their activities.

Once Lily was confident that I had grasped the basics, we began working together. When one of us was selected during a line-up, the other would join the tour to explain that it was my first day in training, offering assistance as needed. Despite Lily's support, I still battled nervousness. Convincing customers to invest their hard-earned money in me was a daunting task since I was brand new.

Upon sharing my concerns with Lily, she advised me to consult with the more experienced girls to gain insight into different negotiating styles. These conversations helped me develop my own techniques, providing a safety net until I felt comfortable negotiating independently. The most challenging part was waiting in the parlor and standing in line, hoping to be chosen. It made me question why some customers didn't select me, and I took it very personal.

Before I knew it my two weeks were over, and it was time to go home. I packed up my room and filled my trunks with the stuff I would be leaving for the next time, loaded my car with the stuff I was taking home, and off I went back to California. The drive home was so much easier than driving all the way back from Los Angeles, and I was home in no time.

The first thing Hans said to me was, "Hey, baby, tell me how much you enjoyed being a whore." It shocked me to hear him say this at first, but in reality, that's exactly what I was, and Hans almost seemed proud.

Hans eagerly listened to every detail of my trip, despite our frequent phone calls after each session. Over dinner, I shared stories about the girls I met, the appointments I booked, the appointment-booking process, and the message board and forum I joined as part of my responsibilities.

After dinner, Hans asked for an intimate conversation with me discussing my experiences with these men while he indulged in his fantasies. Despite his apparent enthusiasm, I couldn't shake the guilt of talking about being with other men. Hans was accepting of my profession, but I was starting to yearn for a more traditional, closed relationship.

Since I had made a decent amount of money on that first trip, we decided I didn't need to make a trip to LA that month. I called my agent and told him I was going to take a break from films and work only at the Ranch. The money was so much better, and it was also cheaper for me to stay at the Ranch than to book a hotel or rent a room from a friend.

Before I returned to the Ranch, it was decided for me to transition out of movies and work solely as a "whore", as Hans so proudly announced. Yes, that's what I was, a Whore, a Hooker, a Prostitute, a Harlot. Whatever my title, I tried very hard not to let it bother me.

◆━━━━━━━━━━━━━━━━◆

I had been doing my two-week trips to the Ranch for nearly four months and things had become pretty routine. I also started a workout routine since we had a gym in the back part of the house, as I was determined to get healthier.

While I was out of town, Hans still expected me to follow certain rules that he had set in place. I was still supposed to call him 'Sir' whenever we talked on the phone, and he always wanted me to send detailed messages about each of my sessions. I found it challenging to comply with these rules while focusing on work, so I decided to end the dynamic.

I needed him to understand, so I tried to explain, "I am open to maintaining a specific dynamic in the bedroom to please you, but Hans, the additional rules and the way you treat me has become overwhelming, and they need to stop."

I could tell he was angry, but he didn't yell. In fact, he agreed, and then he announced, "Amanda, I have a surprise for you. I decided to buy you something, and I think you'll really like it."

Who was I to refuse such a gesture? That's when I subtly started hinting how much I'd love to have my own laptop. I shared the news with two of my friends so that when Hans gave it to me, they would be surprised, too.

One day during my trip, I called Hans and inadvertently learned that he was shopping, which he quickly down played to preserve the surprise element. But, from all the noises in the background, it was pretty clear to me that he was getting me a laptop!

By now, I had adjusted to working long shifts during the week and also on weekends. I worked the graveyard shift, so I typically slept until late morning. However, on the last morning of my September trip, I was awakened by a call from the cashier, asking about insurance for my car.

I rushed out to the parking lot and discovered that a camper shell from a gentleman's truck had been picked up by the wind, and it damaged my car's front fender and hood.

After a frustrating hour on the phone with the insurance

company, they agreed to tow my car to the repair shop. I had to get a friend to give me a ride back to California while they waited for replacement parts, and Hans agreed to drive me back once the car was fixed.

Hans even had the audacity to tell me I should try and convince my friend who gave me the ride to join us in the bedroom. Not wanting to do it, I told him she said she was too tired.

Over the next few days, I secretly searched our house for the laptop that I thought Hans had gotten me, but I never found it.

One evening, Hans asked me, "How come you haven't mentioned your surprise? Don't you want to know what it is?"

That's when I told him, "I've been trying to find it ever since I came home! I've looked everywhere," I confessed. "But if you want to give it to me, I will gladly take it!"

I assumed he'd leave the room to retrieve the laptop, given its size, but instead he followed me. Playfully, he smacked my bottom, and I reciprocated which lead to a playful wrestling match.

Then to my ultimate surprise, he knelt in front of me on one knee, and he reached in his pocket and pulled out a small box. I quickly covered my gaping mouth and whispered to myself, 'Oh my gosh, he's proposing!'

When he did, I was overjoyed with tears streaming down my face. All I ever wanted was for him to truly love me, and this was the most encouraging proof I could have ever asked for.

And, of course, I said, "Yes!" Then I reached up with both my hands on either side of his face, and I kissed him. Afterwards, I admitted that he caught me off guard because I had expected a laptop.

He explained with a grin, "That was all part of my plan, pretending to be at the electronics store when I was actually at the jewelry store."

Like any newly engaged woman, I immediately sent a mass text with a picture of my new ring on my finger. Most of our friends responded with typical "Congratulations!" "So happy for you both!" "When is the big day?"

However, my family's responses were a mixture of good and not so good, with some making light of it all. At the time, I was crushed that they weren't as thrilled for me as I had hoped. But, as I see it all today through different eyes, I'm surprised they responded at all. They were so upset and so concerned for my wellbeing, and I really couldn't blame them at all.

However, at the time, I was disheartened. I asked Hans if he had asked my dad for permission to marry me. Hans confirmed that he had, and that my dad had agreed, "On the condition that she makes some changes in her life."

It made sense, considering how much my family disapproved of certain aspects of my life. Their disappointment dampened my joy, but I figured I would make some changes after the wedding, as I sincerely (but foolishly) believed that Hans would not want to share his life with someone who wasn't aligned with his values.

I also hoped my family would come around once we set the date and they knew it was for real. (I may have even slipped in a prayer out of desperation); after all, I was their oldest daughter and the first to be getting married.

12

Partying for the Holidays

The following weekend, Hans and I threw a grand engagement party, and we invited all of our friends, and Hans' family, too. Hans' younger sister and I even made shirts for potential members of the wedding party. The night was filled with dancing and festivities, and it ended on a heartfelt toast from Hans' step dad and our best man.

All of our guests left early to let us enjoy the rest of the night together. We made plans to host a Halloween party, and everyone from the engagement party would be invited. We set the date for the party after my next trip to the Ranch, giving us time to prepare the house, choose costumes, and save money for food and drinks.

In October I returned to the Ranch, and I wasted no time flaunting my engagement ring to all the girls, and sharing the exciting details. It was a breath of fresh air, because my family still had not shared my enthusiasm. But I refused to let it dampen my joy. My happiness radiated, and this trip turned out to be one of the best.

I had more clients than usual for those two weeks, and I returned with several thousand dollars more in my pocket. I even had a local seamstress create a custom Halloween costume for me for our upcoming party.

On slower nights, the girls and I browsed wedding websites, selecting themes, dresses, and watching Halloween movies together. We even dressed up and decorated the house for Halloween. Before I knew it, my trip was over, and it was time to head home and prepare for the big Halloween party.

Although things seemed better from the outside looking in, I knew that I was being embraced by the devil himself. I didn't care about much of anything except making money and keeping Hans happy so I wouldn't have to stoop so low to perform in his sick make-believe world.

Meanwhile, in my work life, I had to strike a balance between being assertive and not letting clients take advantage of me. I needed to be both tough and compassionate. I also formed close bonds with some of the other girls. When we weren't working, we'd spend time together supporting and motivating each other. Life in Carson City was finally beginning to stabilize, and I was making a very decent living.

One friend in particular, Serenity, became my confidante and partner in navigating our unique profession. We worked together to learn and negotiate various aspects of our work, even though our schedules didn't always align.

My experiences during this time were challenging, but they also shaped me in many ways. I learned the importance of self-respect and maintaining healthy boundaries in relationships, both personal and professional.

The morning of the Halloween party, a girlfriend and I had an appointment at the bridal store for me to try on dresses while Hans and his friend decorated the house.

After our appointment, we stopped by the store to buy snacks and refreshments. We ended up spending a few hundred dollars on supplies and decorations, but it was all going to be worth it. We knew that the people would talk about this party for a very long time.

She and I went upstairs to get dressed as the boys finished up the final touches. Our party was by invitation-only this year to avoid unnecessary drama, so we made sure that everyone coming had RSVP'd ahead of time and submitted their planned costume. This way, we knew if you weren't dressed as a superhero, you weren't on the guest list and would be asked to leave. It worked out well too; we only had to use the list once or twice.

The party was so much fun, just being surrounded by our friends was always a good time. Everyone was enjoying themselves, playing games, and socializing. The girls were having fun with energy drink shots, so we were all wide awake and enjoying ourselves entertaining the guests and making memories.

The next trip to the Ranch was slow due to bad weather, so us girls spent most of the time indoors, watching movies and browsing the internet. We used the time to plan for the wedding, looking for cost-effective ideas and themes.

For my twenty-first birthday, Hans and I went to Carson City to celebrate with some of my friends at the Ranch. I barely noticed that my family wasn't there to celebrate with me as my friends and Hans did their best to make it as memorable as they could.

After Gran took me to my first casino, we headed back home. Then a few days later I headed back to the Ranch, but the weather was challenging once again, and business was slow. When my two weeks were over, I headed for home.

On Christmas, Hans and I spent most of the day with his family. I didn't spend much time with my family as they were still having reservations about us getting married, and they made it a point to tell me every time we talked. It was a very difficult time for me, but I tried hard to understand their concerns.

I ended up having to celebrate New Year's Eve at the Ranch

as the weather made it difficult for us to travel. So, we opened a bottle of champagne and raised our glasses as we toasted to another New Year in hopes that it would be a much better year for everyone. However, it didn't start out that way at all.

In early January, my car was repossessed due to missed payments, and we had to pay fines and penalties to get it back. There was still so much to do for our wedding and things we needed to pay for, and the unexpected expense of the car put added stress and pressure on both of us.

Had I been a praying person like I used to be so long ago, I would have dropped to my knees and begged God to help. But as it turned out, I didn't have to. Maybe there was still some "Higher Power" watching over me and knew what I needed, and He granted me my heart's desire.

Shortly after my car was retrieved, some of us girls from the Ranch were invited to the upcoming Super Bowl party which was an answer for all of us to earn some extra money. With the experience I've had over the few years I'd been doing this, I knew what was necessary in order to make more money, and our shows improved greatly. We even auctioned off a signed football after the game.

After the very successful Super Bowl party, we all went out to dinner with the Super Bowl hosts, and afterwards we went our separate ways and returned to our "home" away from home.

13

Family Isn't Always Blood

With the money I earned at the Super Bowl bash, we managed to catch up on all our bills. Our lease was ending, and without Hans working again we couldn't afford to extend it. Fortunately, one of our friends told us that he had a spare room in his house and offered it to us, so we moved in with him.

This arrangement worked well because he owned the house, and our dogs all got along. We didn't have to worry about finding a new place that would accept our pit bulls due to strict pet policies.

I continued to work at the Ranch, and Hans began searching for a new job since the Ranch's customers were affected by the weather. The extra money I brought in from the Super Bowl shows didn't last long once I started paying off some of the more urgent things concerning the wedding. Suddenly, once again we were dealing with ongoing financial strain, which added to my stress and depression. I was struggling with my weight trying various methods to fit perfectly into my wedding dress, but it felt like my weight was tied to my emotional state.

During my time at the Ranch, Lily, Serenity and I devoted most of our free time to wedding preparations. Fortunately, there was a bridal store chain in both Reno and Sacramento, so that I could involve most of my bridesmaids in choosing dresses.

Even though Gran and Aunt Ellie were able to join us in picking out dresses, I longed for the presence of my mom and sisters. This was not how I had pictured my wedding day planning as a little girl.

With financial assistance limited, I was so grateful when both Lily and Serenity lent me their contribution by purchasing various wedding items that were still needed. Some of the other girls at the Ranch also felt a sense of obligation to help me because we were like family, and they included me in several upcoming parties to ensure that I could earn some extra money.

Not all families get along though, right? One morning after finishing up a session, I went back to Lily's room. She and I used my room for sessions and hers for relaxing. I slammed my water, and a few hours later, I came to the scary conclusion that someone had laced my drink with Oxycodone. Apparently, the girls who did it thought it was Lily's drink, not mine. So much for the Ranch being a safer and more controlled environment.

In the following months, I split my time between working at the Ranch and organizing the wedding. My Aunt Ellie and Granny, who lived in the area, did their best to support me. Despite my strained relationship with my immediate family, my aunt and Granny wanted me to know that I still had their love and support. This caused some tension with my parents, but the two of them reassured me that things would improve over time.

I also had reached out to my dad's extended family, hoping for similar support, but my uncle's response was hurtful and disheartening, leading me to distance myself from my dad's side of the family for a while.

One evening, I met with my aunt, Granny, and my cousin at the bridal store, where they helped me select my bridal and bridesmaid dresses. It was challenging to plan the wedding without my immediate family's involvement, but their laughter and support helped me to feel less alone.

Back at home, I was coordinating wedding plans with the girls in Sacramento, with minimal assistance from either of our families. My youngest sister joined me for my final dress fitting, and we had a wonderful time, despite her reservations about the marriage. Hans' family wasn't very involved either, as his mother disapproved of inviting some of her relatives due to a recent family dispute.

Fortunately, while I was at work, Hans got to know our neighbors across the street, Riley, Shane, and their youngest son Xavier. We quickly became friends and formed a close-knit group. Riley became a maternal figure in my life, providing much-needed support during a stressful time. Our gatherings helped us forget wedding-related stress and enjoy the company of our new friends.

One night, Xavier introduced us to his older brother Miguel, who was on leave from the Army. He joined us briefly for a few drinks, and then he left to meet up with some of his friends.

Although I couldn't understand at the time why all my family and friends were being so cruel and distant. All I wanted from them was to be happy for me. But they couldn't, for they could see the treacherous path I was on, and they knew I was heading straight for hell. I was too far gone at the time to see clearly what they already knew.

Years later, when I finally came to my senses and left the sex industry, I begged forgiveness from all my family. I was so caught up in the sin of it all that I couldn't see "the forest for the trees".

Thankfully they all loved me enough to forgive and forget. However, at this time, I still had some pain to endure and some major things to let go of. And the most difficult would be my relationship with Hans, because of the control he had over me.

14

~~~~~~~~~

One Night Changed Everything

Hans got a new job at a party supply store, but unfortunately it wasn't paying enough. We just weren't able to make ends meet. And with my decreasing income at the Ranch, it was time to find other options.

I shared my concerns with a few girls at the Ranch, and they suggested a few ideas that I'd have to think about. In the meantime, they helped me bring in a little money by working a few parties/ sessions with them on the side. There was still so much to do for the wedding and without any assistance from either of our parents, we weren't sure how we were going to pay for so many necessary things like our rings, the cake, the catering, and the list went on.

Luckily for us, Hans' best man was willing to pay for his bachelor party in Las Vegas, and Hans and our roommate spent four days in Vegas doing anything they wanted while I went to work.

One of the appointments was with a nice couple who were looking to spice things up on their trip around the United States. They were able to sell their company and retire early, and both of them thought that a stop at the Bunny Ranch would be a nice way to mix things up without having to worry about another woman breaking them up.

After our first meeting, we settled on $10,000 for the next twelve hours. The manager let us use the house in the back by the pool so that we weren't interrupted by the general noise from the main house, and we could have our privacy. I brought Lily into the party for a few hours, and the four of us went to dinner.

Afterward, we all spent time in the heated pool, then the four of us had another "group" session before they retired to take a nap. Lily and I headed back inside the main house and let them sleep in private.

We ended up only spending two thirds of the twelve allotted hours the couple had booked with us because I noticed the woman was starting to have second thoughts. It was obvious the two of them wanted some alone time together without us.

The next morning, I took them to the main house for breakfast and to meet the owner. I said my goodbyes and they went on their way as happy as could be.

Since the Ranch keeps half of the money, and I had them pay Lily separately, I ended up taking home $5,000 from that one appointment. The rest of the trip was uneventful, and that one overnight appointment was my saving grace fi nancially, as I was now able to pay off my wedding ring and the rest of our venue.

There was still a balance on the cake and on my dress, but luckily, Serenity paid off the cake and my good friends at the Ranch pitched in to pay off the rest of my dress. They were my family.

The next morning Lily and I went to my grandparents' anniversary barbeque. This was the first time in years that I had seen most of my family, and it ended up being a very good day.

While inside helping my aunts with the food tray, they asked me why I didn't send them invitations to the wedding. I was taken aback at first, but then I gathered my thoughts and explained.

"Because my parents made it very clear that if I was going to continue in the sex industry, none of my family would want to come to my wedding because they would not support a marriage like mine," I told them through my tears.

They both responded sweetly, "We wished you had sent the invitations and given us the chance to decide for ourselves, because no matt er what, Amanda, we all still love you." Of course, this made me cry even more.

After we took several family pictures, I told them all how wonderful it was to see them, but it was time for us to leave. We said our goodbyes, and most everyone said they loved me and that they would continue to pray for me to come back to them. My heart was so full, and I truly rejoiced at their words.

My parents and sisters walked us to the car. Then my sisters each gave me a big hug and said, "We miss you, Manda." Then they headed back to the house. My parents stayed behind to talk for a few minutes. Lily said goodbye and got into the car so that I could have my privacy with them.

I hugged and kissed them both, then I asked, "Will you be coming to the wedding?" because I still had hopes that they would show up. But those hopes were quickly crushed as my dad shared once again, "We can't Amanda. I hope you will understand some day. We just can't stand up in front of everyone and God, and admit that we are proud of our daughter, the prostitute." His words were painful to hear, but it was the truth.

Of course, I started crying again, and my mom whispered, "Honey, if you quit the industry entirely and wait until December, your father and I will gladly pay for you to have a small wedding."

With my wedding only a few weeks away, I couldn't quit being what I was yet, because we weren't making enough money for me to stop. With this reality, I said goodbye again and thanked them.

On the way back to the Ranch, Lily spent the entire trip trying to calm me down, reassuring me to, "Give it time, honey. They will come around." As we were pulling in, Hans called me to tell me he was back from Vegas. Not knowing he was on speaker phone, he ended up complaining about Lily, which really upset her.

The next morning my cousin Jeremiah reached out and asked if he could stop by so we could talk. Of course, I agreed, and we ended up having breakfast together.

Jeremiah tried to understand my side of how I ended up in the industry, and to see if there was anything he could do to help me get out. He was so sweet, but I explained, "At this point, there's nothing you can do, Jer. It's the money that keeps me here, and that's why I have to stay. If I quit, our bills won't get paid." He was so kind to hear me out, but I don't think he understood my situation.

"Please don't worry, Jeremiah. I have no intentions of staying in this polluted industry after Hans and I are married. I want out, but I can't right now!" My cousin wasn't excited about my answer, but he was happy that I had plans to stop in the future.

We went our separate ways with him hugging me and praying for my safety. I was so grateful to have him on my side, even though I was still so far away from the life I used to know.

God had given me a glimmer of hope that I had not truly lost all my family.

15

When It Rains It Pours

The next weekend, Lily and I were supposed to have my bachelorette party in San Francisco, but we received a call from one of our high-paying clients who wanted to meet us. The Ranch owner gave us permission to meet him in San Francisco instead of him coming to Carson City, as he had given us his credit card information over the phone to cover our expenses.

I met Lily at the hotel that afternoon just before our client arrived, and she was acting strange and distant, but she didn't want to share what was bothering her.

After we finished with our appointment, a few of our friends joined us at the hotel. We started to go downstairs, when suddenly,

Lily stood and said she needed to get more towels from downstairs because we had used them all. She left in a hurry.

After waiting an hour with no sign of her or her response to our calls, she finally answered the phone. That's when she blindsided me with her words, "Amanda, I'm not coming back, and I never want to see you or talk to you again. And by the way, I'm no longer your maid of honor either! Have a nice life!" she said, then she hung up. She never said why, and to this day I still don't know, but I can assume it had something to do with that speaker phone incident.

My friends could tell something was wrong by the look on my face. I was in shock. I told them what she said, and then I started crying. I felt terrible; I had just lost my best friend, my maid of honor, and now my bachelorette party was ruined.

Lily had been the one who put this party together. She knew where all the fun spots were, and she was the one who made and paid for all the reservations. It was supposed to be a surprise, so she never told anyone where we were going, not even my friends... SURPRISE!

However, my friends refused to let her win. Despite the unfortunate turn of events, they all encouraged me to enjoy the night, and so we did. We found a place to eat, visited a strip club briefly but left soon after arriving, and stopped at a few bars. None of us wanted to be bothered by strangers, so after a while, we went back to the hotel. We picked up some drinks and snacks from a liquor store and spent the rest of the night watching cartoons, chatting, and having a surprisingly enjoyable time.

The next day I headed back to Carson City to continue my bachelorette weekend at a club in Reno with my girlfriends from the Ranch. We had a great time, enjoying VIP treatment, dancing, and making memorable moments.

As the wedding date approached, there were several last-minute challenges. One of my bridesmaids had to bow out due to a convention she had to attend in Los Angeles, so I asked another girl to step in as a junior bridesmaid, and she was happy to be included.

Then one of the groomsmen and his family threatened to drop out as well, but I resolved the situation by paying for their expenses. On top of all this, our original officiant informed me that he couldn't perform the ceremony due to personal reasons, so I had to find a replacement.

On the day before the wedding, I picked up my wedding dress, but I had trouble getting it to zip up. Nicki, a member of the wedding party, said she could help modify the dress into a corseted back style to ensure it fit perfectly.

The evening before the wedding, we worked on the last-minute preparations and had the rehearsal dinner, where his mother caused more stress by arriving late, because she was getting her nails done and only showed because I threatened to uninvite her to the wedding.

While the boys partied at home, us girls spent the night modifying the dress and getting little sleep. The next morning, we got up early, had breakfast, and headed to the hair salon.

I called Hans to make sure he and his best man were ready for their appointments, but they were still recovering from partying late into the night, which added to the pre-wedding chaos.

It truly does seem that when it rains, it pours. However, I wasn't going to let this or anything else upset me or stress me out. This was my wedding day, and it was going to be perfect, come hell or high water if need be!

16

How Many Red Flags Did I Need?

By the time we arrived at the salon, I was grateful that I had calmed down and was ready to be pampered. The stylist asked how I wanted my hair, and I told him I wanted it all up and in big loose curls with my tiara. It took him two very stressful tries, but he finally understood.

While he was fixing my hair, I received a phone call from my soon-to-be mother-in-law saying they had finished decorating, but she decided not to decorate the head table because she didn't know what I wanted it to look like. She left it for me to do later.

I hadn't planned to go to the venue prior to the ceremony, and my nerves began to crumble as panic set in. I knew there was no way to fix this without making a scene. That's when I called my Aunt Ellie.

She had to drop her husband off early because he was our DJ and he had to set up all his DJ equipment. I asked my aunt if she could please decorate the head table for me. Aunt Ellie heard the stress in my voice, and she told me that she would take care of it and everything would be fine, "Now, go enjoy being pampered and get your hair done. This is your day, sweet one." Finally I could breathe.

Before I had a chance to take in another breath, the photographer called to let me know he was just leaving and that he would see me soon. He wasn't from around here, so I asked if he needed directions. You could have knocked me over with a feather when he informed me that he was just leaving LA! Oh dear.

This meant he would be getting into town only moments before the ceremony began, which meant I probably wouldn't get any of the "getting ready for the wedding" poses that I had requested. It was disappointing, and I started to worry because things were starting to fall apart. Thank heavens I had Gran by my side, and together we came up with a solution.

We asked everyone if they would take candid shots throughout the day while they helped get everything ready, so that we would have some pictures from before the ceremony instead of having none.

When the hairdresser finished with my hair, it was exactly what I wanted, and I was so relieved. My tiara was shining, I had a head full of beautiful curls, and my hairdresser was ready to show Gran how to put on my veil. My Gran insisted that she knew how to do the veil, so we had left the veil at the hotel that morning.

This was not going to work for the hairdresser, so after a brief disagreement, my Gran made a quick trip to the local craft store to buy a second veil just to calm him down.

The hairdresser then showed her exactly where it had to go. We took pictures of all the girls posing with the stylists and then headed back to the hotel to get dressed and do our makeup.

Gran stopped at the sandwich shop and told me I had to eat something, even though I had no appetite. I gave in and had half a sandwich and a cookie. On the way home, the florist called, saying she had left all the flowers at my house to keep them in the cooler. Hans had already left to go get everything set up at the venue, so we had to stop off at the house and take the flowers to the hotel with us, ensuring that they would all get to the wedding party.

When we finally made it back to the room, Nicki had already finished the makeup of the two bridesmaids who hadn't gone to the salon with us. Now it was my turn.

As I sat there finally able to relax and have my makeup done, the bakery called and asked if they could show up a half-hour later than we had originally planned. I agreed, thinking they needed to make some last-minute touches. My maid of honor commented on how amazed she was that I remained so calm despite the little things not falling into place.

As Nicki had done my makeup many times before, she knew exactly what I wanted, and it turned out perfect. She had to do some last-minute touch-ups on herself, so I added a little bit of blush and shimmer to my adorable flower girl and placed her tiara in her hair.

Once she was done, it was time for her and my aunt to head to the venue so we could get my dress on and have more space in the room. My aunt took all the flowers for the boys in the wedding party and for my in-laws.

As I started to put on my dress, I suddenly felt extremely overwhelmed and sick to my stomach. My nerves hit me like a truck load of bricks when I realized that this was it; I was getting married!

With all the running around that day and trying not to let the little things stress me out, I had forced myself to ignore my nerves. But there was no holding them back now. Don't get me wrong, I was happy that my wedding day was here, but it hit me hard when I realized that most of the blood relatives I invited had all been in the same room with me until just a few minutes ago!

Deep inside I still had such high hopes that my parents would have changed their minds and been there for me, but they weren't, and it hurt. Since my dad wouldn't be coming, I wasn't sure who would be walking me down the aisle and give me away, until my dear friend and father figure Arthur said he'd be honored to do it, to which I was very grateful.

I took a minute and sat on the bed to collect myself. In fact, I almost thought I should say a prayer, but then why would God even listen? I hadn't talked to Him for so long, and it's almost certain that He would not have approved of Hans and me getting married either. So there was no need for me to pray.

When I felt like I wasn't going to be sick, I stood up. Then I stepped into my dress, and with the help of several people, it was tied, and they helped me put on my necklace.

Now it was time to check my "something borrowed, something blue, something old, and something new." As my something old, I wore my Gran's earrings. My necklace was my something new, my toes were painted blue, and I had a pair of blue panties to wear under my dress, but I didn't know what my something borrowed would be yet.

When I walked across the room to get my heels, Serenity stopped me. She informed me, "Oh no, Amanda, your blue undies are showing right through your dress and that is not cool! You need to take them off!"

I was panic stricken because it was the only pair I had. What was I going to do? I started shaking and almost burst into tears, but then Serenity came to the rescue again.

"Wait, you can wear mine. I just put them on so they're clean. Plus, now you have your something borrowed!" she announced proudly.

Catching my breath once again, I quickly changed into Serenity's underwear and then put on my heels. I was ready at last! First for some quick photos with each of my bridesmaids, and then for my vows.

I was on my last nerve when I received another call from the photographer letting me know he was in town, but first he needed to stop at the store for batteries. I looked at the clock on the wall and was immediately irritated. The ceremony was supposed to start in ten minutes! I wanted to scream.

I didn't know if I would even have a photographer here to take my wedding pictures, but it was too late to worry about that now. Not wanting to dwell on the situation and stress myself out more, I told everyone it was time to figure out the transportation for the wedding party.

We quickly sorted out who would be riding with whom and headed to the parking lot, when I realized, in all the commotion that I had forgotten my veil. We sent Serenity's boyfriend back to the room to get it since he was the only one not in heels or a wheelchair.

After triple-checking that we now had everything, we headed

to the venue only ten minutes behind schedule. It actually ended up working just fine because the groomsmen had been struggling with the sudden wind gusts that was blowing the aisle runner all over, and people's shoes going through it. Nothing was going according to schedule, so it left us with enough time to snap some of the pre-ceremony shots that I had wanted.

As soon as I got there, the photographer rushed over and started snapping pictures, trying to make up for what he had missed. We opted out of the aisle runner and started the ceremony. It was only thirty minutes late, though no one seemed to mind.

The wedding party lined up and everyone was ready to walk to the songs we had picked out. Our ceremony music was not your typical music for a wedding, and as soon as it started, you could see the surprise on everyone's faces.

I stood hidden behind a patch of large bushes so my groom couldn't see me. I heard it was bad luck for the groom to see the bride prior to the ceremony, and I just couldn't take any chances!

After handing his ring to the best man, I watched as the man I was about to call my husband, walked down the aisle to "Dead Man Walking." To us that song seemed appropriate since this was his last walk as a single man, and we thought it was amusing.

Next, my gorgeous bridesmaids partnered with their designated groomsmen. Then pair by pair, my very handsome wedding party took their turns walking down the aisle to "All

My Friends Are Criminals." Not that they were criminals (well, except for one groomsman.) This song felt fitting for our wedding as well, since my family didn't approve of the marriage, and here was this group of misfit friends willing to defy my parents' wishes.

Then it was time for my favorite part of the wedding party, the flower girl and the ring bearer. I picked out their song and didn't let Hans have any say in it because "Itty Bitty" was a special song to my little cousin, who was the flower girl, and she used to sing in the car with my Aunt Ellie. The problem now was that the ring bearer wanted nothing to do with the flower girl. He had his heart set on walking with his Papa (Arthur), which wasn't going to happen since his Papa was the one walking me down the aisle in place of my father.

After a few minutes of trying to convince the little guy that he didn't need to walk with his Papa, and finally having his grandma bribe him with a promise of candy, he ran down the aisle to his dad who was now out of the groomsmen line. From where I stood, it was pretty funny, and also to be expected of a two-year-old.

Then I realized it was my turn to walk the aisle, so I quickly composed myself and took the hand of the man who would give me away.

Despite the numerous red flags, which I tried hard not to notice, the day was almost over, and soon I would be a married woman.

17

Wedding Day Blues

This was it! Our wedding day! Suddenly, a million thoughts flooded my mind. I was about to take my last walk ever as a single woman. I wondered where my parents were and why they didn't want to be here with me on my big day. Would they ever support this marriage? Was I really doing this? Then, finally, I looked up into sweet Arthur's smiling face, and I heard him say, "It's our turn, honey. Let's do this."

Although it would have been funny to see me running on the grass in my six-inch heels with Arthur beside me using his cane, we took our time and carefully walked toward my soon-to-be groom. In his nervousness, Arthur had forgotten to lift my veil and instead, just shook Hans' hand before quickly making his way to his seat.

Giggling at Arthur's nervousness, I whispered to Hans to lift my veil. My roommate Derrick (who was officiating our wedding) then asked, "Who will present Amanda to be married today?" Knowing how much I wanted my dad to be the one to answer, Arthur quickly shouted, "Her friends and I do."

Derrick continued with the ceremony, nervously reciting it just as he had rehearsed it. He talked about what a great couple we were, even if we weren't the most traditional couple. To be honest, I stopped paying attention to what he was saying because I didn't want to start crying. I kept looking over at Hans, smiling, and then back to Derrick, who was now tearing up a bit himself. I gazed down at the flowers in my hand, wishing I had remembered to grab some Kleenex.

Then it happened; it was time to exchange our vows. I handed my bouquet to my maid of honor, as Hans gently took my hand. The rest of the ceremony was a blur as each step toward the finale grew closer. Rings were placed on our hands, and the promises of "I do" were spoken.

The next thing I heard was, "I now pronounce you man and wife. Hans, you may kiss your bride." Much to everyone's surprise, we didn't have an overly long or romantic kiss. But I didn't even notice. I was just so relieved that it was over.

Derrick announced the "happy couple" to the crowd for the first time as Mr. and Mrs. Then we made our way over the bridge, pausing for just a moment to snap a quick picture, and start the reception line. The two of us stood there watching our wedding party walk over the bridge two by two, briefly hugging us, then joining us in line.

It was an amazing and heartwarming feeling as everyone hugged and congratulated us as they walked past. Hans' aunt was crying and wouldn't stop hugging me because she was so excited that I was officially a part of her family.

After all the pictures were taken, Hans and I made our way over to the head table so we could make our "thank you" speech and start the toasts.

My uncle started the speeches for us with a cute and comedic toast to lighten the mood. He then thanked everyone for coming as he filled in for the speech I had expected from my dad on my wedding day.

Our best man Lee and his wife Hana, who was also our maid of honor, made their speeches full of laughs, joyful congratulations, and excitement about them spending time with us at the beach in San Diego while we were on our honeymoon. Hans' dad and step dad followed with loving and congratulatory toasts. Next came a few of our friends, and ending with his teary-eyed aunt's bittersweet welcome to the family speech.

I felt the butterflies starting to flutter in my stomach as my uncle made his way back towards our table with the microphone so that my husband and I could give the traditional "thank-you-for-coming" toast. I had expected Hans to be the one to make the toast, but to my surprise, he didn't have much to say and left it up to me.

I had only gotten a few seconds into the speech, before I started fighting back the tears. I mentioned how much it meant to us that everyone who was there had shown up to support us, even when many had not.

I wanted to keep going and end it with a beautiful "thank you" to everyone, but I couldn't talk any longer without thinking about my non supportive parents. Luckily, my uncle was watching me closely and quickly stepped in and took over the toast, announcing it was time to cut the cake.

The rest of the evening went well, and everyone seemed to have a good time. Along with the cake cutting, there was champagne, and dancing, and the traditional garter and bouquet toss. Then before I knew it, the night was over. It was time to pack the gifts into the car and head to our honeymoon suite, which the girls from the Ranch had kindly gifted us.

Hans and I said our goodbyes to the few guests that were left, and Hans and his groomsmen started putting gifts into the car. I was so exhausted, I just sat in the car talking with my bridesmaids, and before I knew it, I was sobbing. It just hit me again how much I missed having my family there, on my one and only wedding day.

When I finally ran out of tears and all the gifts were packed, it was time for us to leave. I hugged everyone and thanked them for their comforting, encouraging words, and with the promise that I was feeling better, though deep inside I was still struggling.

Lee and Hana were staying at the same hotel with us since we were carpooling down to San Diego together the following morning. I was so exhausted from all the craziness of the day and the lack of sleep the night before, I fell asleep ten minutes into the forty-five-minute car ride to the hotel.

When we arrived, we checked into our rooms, and we all agreed that we would meet back up in the lobby around eight the next morning. Then we went our separate ways.

As Hans and I approached our wedding suite door, I looked over at my husband and asked, "Aren't you going to carry me across the threshold?" He was slow to respond, and it wasn't what I expected at all.

He shook his head and said, "No, I don't think so." When I asked him why, he shrugged and said, "Because I really don't feel like it." What a great start to a romantic and joy-filled honeymoon!

We made our way into the gorgeous suite overlooking the capital, and the first thing I did was take a few pictures to remember this wonderful gift from the girls.

Now, based on what you have read so far, you'd think that the night would have been filled with sweet words of love and intimacy, but that was not the case.

We sealed our vows quickly, and then we both rolled to the center of the bed. He said he loved me and that he was happy to finally call me his wife. I said, "I love you, too." Then we both fell asleep.

It was far from magical, and a bit disappointing, but it was definitely memorable. And for this, I was content.

18

Honeymoon Adventures Await

I was in a deep sleep when suddenly I was jolted awake by the sound of a cell phone ringing. At first I thought it was the alarm going off, but when I opened my eyes, the sun was shining brightly through the sliding glass door, and I quickly realized it was much later than either of us thought. We had slept through the "round two" alarm on Hans' cellphone, and it was already after eight!

Disoriented and half asleep, we both jumped out of bed like two crazy people, made ourselves semi presentable and packed up what little we had. Then we flew out the door.

A delicious continental breakfast was waiting for us in the

lobby, and we were definitely hungry. We took our time enjoying every bite before heading to Lee's parent's house in the Bay. I had never met his parents, but since he and Hans had grown up together, we figured it would be a great start to our vacation. Plus, it was by the beach, so how could it not be wonderful?

When our stomachs were full, it was time to hit the road. Luckily for us, there wasn't much traffic since it was Sunday morning, so the drive was a short and easy one out to the Bay. The boys made sure we drove next to the water for a few minutes so we could see how pretty the view was before seeing nothing but open fields on the way to San Diego.

We had a wonderful visit with Lee's parents, filled with home-cooked foods and reminiscing about when the boys were little. But knowing we still had a long drive ahead of us, we said our goodbyes and thanked them and continued our adventure.

Lee and Hana told us not to worry about booking a hotel in San Diego because they had a spare room, and we were welcome to use it. It was a relief to know we didn't have to spend any more money on a hotel room.

Once we got to their apartment, we did a quick unload of our luggage, and we grabbed something to eat since we were all too tired to try and cook something ourselves. We went to this little Mexican restaurant down the street and made plans to go to the beach the following afternoon, and then to Sea World the next day.

The following morning, we woke up to the smell of Hana making her special chocolate chip pancakes. After breakfast, we packed up a bag for the beach and made our way down the street to enjoy a few hours in the sun. Luckily for us, Lee didn't have to work that day, and Hana didn't work until later that evening, so it ended up being the four of us going out.

We spent the afternoon playing in the waves, boogie boarding, sunbathing, and burying Lee and Hans in the sand. We ate our picnic lunch on the beach and spent a few more hours in the water before going back to the apartment to get cleaned up so we could go to the boardwalk.

Before we knew it, the night was over, and we headed back to the apartment to get some sleep since we were going to Sea World the next day.

Once again, we woke up to Hana cooking breakfast for us. It was wonderful to be so pampered, and we were grateful not to have to spend money eating out. We ate quickly so we could get to Sea World before it got too hot, and the lines got too long.

The day was fun and memorable as the four of us rode all the rides, checked out all the sea creatures, and took a bunch of pictures together. Later that afternoon, Lee got a call from a coworker, who asked if he and Hana could house sit for him, which meant that we would get the apartment completely to ourselves! Of course, we were excited because it meant we would finally be able to relax. Even though I was tired and not in the mood, Hans pleaded with me to have sex. He said I was his wife now and I was obligated to do it. Not wanting to fight, I reluctantly gave in.

We had dinner at their coworker's house, and I was able to get a hold of my cousin who had gotten us discounted Disneyland tickets. Hans called his boss and took another week off so we could go to Disneyland and visit some other extended family who lived in the area.

When we got back to the apartment, I quickly changed, and we enjoyed a private evening. My cousin's wife was a blossoming photographer, so she offered to take some photos of us. We spent the following afternoon with my cousins on the beach taking our honeymoon portraits. We ended the day with dinner and a round of mini golf, then we headed back to the apartment for the last time.

We had breakfast with Lee and Hana one last time before heading off to visit Hans' grandmother and my great grandfather. It was a few hours out of the way, but we felt it important to see them. We planned to eat lunch with his grandmother in Palm Springs, and though we had heard that Palm Springs was hot, we had no idea just how hot until we got there. Hans' poor grandmother didn't have any air conditioning, so we took her out to lunch instead.

Afterward, we dined with some of my extended family at their house, then we made our way back towards Disneyland. As much as we would have loved to stay longer, we still had a lot of driving to do.

When we got close to Anaheim, I found us the closest, most inexpensive hotel so we could finally lay down, watch some television, and just relax. Even though I was tired and not in the mood, Hans pleaded with me to have sex, saying I was his wife now and I was obligated to do it. Not wanting to fight, I reluctantly gave in.

We spent the next day at Disneyland being little kids again. It almost felt normal, like I belonged there doing things that weren't shameful or embarrassing. We were even given bride and groom hats and they staged pictures of one of the characters marrying us. We also went to the make-believe "City Hall" building, and were given special "Just Married" pins with Disney characters on them. Everything was so special, and everyone seemed to want to be a part of our memory.

It was wonderful being away from everything and everyone, and to be able to let loose and just relax for a while. The whole day was spent doing whatever we wanted, when we wanted. We didn't even mind the long lines or being out in the sun all day.

Hans and I were having so much fun, we lost track of time. When we heard them announce that the park was closing, we made our way through the crowd and back to the hotel to get some rest before our long journey back to reality.

After an uneventful night and morning it was time to leave this Fantasyland, and get back to the lives we had before we left. However, this time it would be as man and wife. What was I thinking?

Honestly, I had deep down wanted the fact we were married now to be the reason we came back and would start a "normal" life.

19

~∾~

Mr. & Mrs. But Not for Long

The next few days were calm and relaxing. Hans went back to work, and I was able to meet up with some of my girlfriends, sharing stories about our honeymoon adventure. Before I knew it, it was time for me to return for my two weeks at the Ranch.

Once again, I packed my bags, said my goodbyes, then headed off to the land of make believe where dreams never come true, and my glass slipper was nowhere to be found.

The drive over was surreal as I found myself thinking about my profession again, and how I would feel being with other men now that I was married. Marriage had always been sacred to me, and I greatly respected the commitment because of what I witnessed at home with my mother and father.

I wasn't sure how all of this was going to play out, or how I could just freely give myself to someone else for payment and think it was okay. I was struggling, but I knew that Hans' income alone could never support us, and I knew, too, that I needed to find a well-paying job before I could retire.

However, just the thought of not being this person I currently had to be gave me great hope. It would take some time to figure it out, but I knew deep down it was what I truly wanted. Unfortunately, I didn't have much time to think about it before I arrived at the Ranch.

As soon as I walked inside, it was time for our weekly meeting and the doctor's visit. Once that was over, the girls were eager to see my wedding pictures and hear all about the honeymoon.

It was heartwarming to know that these people cared enough to be excited for me. Luckily, this trip to the Ranch went without any drama, aside from the usual challenges of living in a house full of girls, and me pretending that this would be my forever job when I knew it wouldn't be for long. I inquired about Lily, but no one had seen or heard from her, so I was able to relax without worrying that she might show up.

Over the next few months, life continued as usual. It was only out of necessity that I continued my trips to the Ranch. However, as I was trying to figure out another line of work, Hans expressed his desire for me to be more submissive in our relationship. I figured since he brought it up, it seemed the perfect time to explain to Hans that I was only comfortable with that dynamic in our bedroom, with just him and me. But it was as if he never heard, and my words evaporated into thin air.

To my surprise, I learned that Hans had met a girl named Sophia, and he wanted me to meet her so she could join us for some "fun". I don't know why I didn't just tell him no, that I was done with all that. I guess bad habits truly were hard to break. Plus, I wasn't really ready to deal with the wrath of Hans at my suggestion.

Hans still had such a hold on me, and I reluctantly agreed to see if I liked her enough to go along with Hans' desires. For now, I had to push away the hope that he would eventually share my desire for an exclusive relationship, and my pursuit of working at a "regular" job someday.

A few days later, Hans invited Sophia to one of our gatherings. She seemed nice enough, and I didn't think much of her joining us for the night. Sadly, I had already been programed for too many years to be submissive to this man and to do whatever he wanted me to do. I knew it would take a miracle for the chains to be broken.

The three of us spent the evening socializing and drinking before retiring to our room. Sophia was submissive, just as Hans desired, so I spent the night watching him take on the dominant role with her, as he had wanted me to do.

It had become clear that Hans had established specific rules for Sophia during the party, leading her to disciplinary actions. The rest of the night was spent with the three of us entwined together until we eventually fell asleep from exhaustion.

The next morning, Sophia left, and I assumed it would be the last time I'd have to see her. I brought the subject up to Hans again about my desire to step away from the Ranch, because the income wasn't as lucrative, and the bills were piling up. But instead of him trying to help me out of the business, he suggested that we contact Serenity and discuss her earlier offer of having our clients come to her home, instead of to the Ranch.

Serenity had explained what being on this website entailed and how it worked logistically. I decided to postpone my trip to the Ranch in September and, instead, head to the Bay to work with Serenity.

The plan was for me to stay with her and her boyfriend at their apartment, where they both would provide guidance to this new adventure for me. Before I left, Derrick expressed his concerns, highlighting its legal risks and lack of protection. I promised him I would be cautious and asked him to keep an eye on Sophia since I had a strange feeling about her.

After a few hours of being stuck in traffic, I finally arrived at

Serenity's apartment. We were excited to have some one-on-one conversations without the constraints of the Ranch. The two of us went out for dinner, walked her dog in the park, and talked for hours.

Once we settled in at the apartment, Serenity showed me how the website worked and explained the safety measures she took to avoid legal issues and dangerous situations. She helped me set up my own ad on the website and get a fake number for call forwarding to my cell. We quickly scheduled appointments for the night since she had already informed her regular clients that I would be joining her that week.

We both dressed up, then we threw on our robes and went into the living room where her boyfriend, Devon, was waiting. Since Serenity and I were handling appointments as a couple, Devon would hide in the other bedroom for safety reasons. We had a few mixed drinks while waiting for the first client to arrive.

When we heard a knock on the door, Devon took the dog and hid in the bedroom so we could let the client in. Serenity reassured me that everything was legitimate, and we would only proceed with what I felt comfortable doing.

Serenity opened the door, hugged her client, and expressed her excitement about him joining us that night. After introducing myself, we started the session by preparing the shower for him. She advised me to cancel the session for safety reasons if a client ever refused a hug at the door. We had a few code words to ensure our safety, and we conducted the session as we would at the Ranch. The prices were lower, because we weren't paying a house fee, which meant the appointment was shorter.

Time passed quickly, and before we knew it, our time with the client was up. We both walked him to the door, thanked him, and expressed our eagerness to see him again. After confirming that I was comfortable enough to continue, we each took a shower and waited for the next client.

Thirty minutes later, there was another knock on the door, signaling round two. This client received the same hug at the door and a trip to the shower. We proceeded with the appointment like we would at the Ranch. The only difference was that he was initially nervous about the presence of an unfamiliar girl. However, we both reassured him that everything was safe, and it was not a setup.

The client eventually relaxed enough to enjoy the session and, as before, we thanked him and headed for a second shower. Instead of scheduling another appointment, the two of us changed the bedding and retired to our separate bedrooms for the night.

I called Hans to say goodnight and give him an update on how the night had gone. He mentioned having lunch with Sophia the next day but assured me that it wouldn't be anything sexual. Given the distance, I took him at his word. We said our "goodnights" then ended the call to get some sleep.

The next few days were filled with shopping, leisurely walks, and ordering takeout as we scheduled appointments throughout the day. Devon wanted to do something nice for us, so he made an appointment for us to get our nails done, and then bought us dinner and a movie.

After several days with many appointments, Serenity and I decided to take time off so that we could just relax. I had earned more in a week than I had during my last two-week trips to the Ranch. I told Serenity that since the money had been so good, I'd be returning in a few weeks to her place instead of going back to the Ranch in November, and she was okay with it.

This new adventure we were exploring wasn't what I had in mind for a new career, but it felt better than being on display in a line up and waiting for someone to choose me.

I also realized that I didn't feel quite as used being this type of whore than being the type of prostitute I had to be at the Ranch.

My heart was still eager not being either someday, though it didn't come as quickly as I hoped it would.

20

Happy News... Not to Be

As much as I loved spending time with Serenity, it was time for me to head home since Hans and I had to be in Reno the next day for Riley and Shane's wedding. I packed up, said my goodbyes, and headed home. After a few hours of being stuck in traffic, I was finally home and so happy to see my dogs. They welcomed me back in sweet dog fashion, and always made me feel loved.

The next few weeks went by too quickly, and soon it was time for another work trip to the Bay. I was excited to see Serenity again but deep inside I hoped for less travel.

On our first day together, Serenity and I had nail appointments and a quick lunch. She suggested we cook more at home during this trip to help me improve my cooking skills, as Hans had mentioned several times that I wasn't very good at it. After planning our meals, we went shopping for all the ingredients we would need. I sent Hans a text and told him that Serenity was teaching me to cook some of his favorite meals, but he never responded.

A few hours later, I called him, and he answered, "I'm sorry, Amanda, I was hanging out with some friends and didn't see your messages. Are you okay?" he asked, but not with much concern.

"Yes, I'm fine. I just wanted to talk to you," I said, trying not to sound as irritated as I was. Something about the situation didn't sit right with me. My instincts told me there might be more to the story, but I couldn't confirm anything from this far away.

The next two days were filled with work appointments and cooking lessons. During one of my calls with Hans, he asked sweetly, "Do you think we could add Sophia to our phone plan because she's facing some financial difficulties and needs to stay in touch with her children? Please, Babe, it would mean a lot."

While I never hesitated before when helping someone in need, I knew this was a bad idea, and I said so, "No, I don't feel comfortable doing this. I'm sorry. Besides we're struggling to pay our own bills." Hans ended the call, and I hung up.

I shared with Serenity what Hans had asked me, and she came up with an idea. "How about we go try our luck in Vegas!" she said, smiling mischievously. Her idea was to take what we were doing here with our "customers" and do it Las Vegas. Before I could change my mind, we were boarding a plane.

After checking into our room and posting our ad, we decided to have drinks by the pool. While enjoying our drinks, our first appointment came through, and we scheduled it for later that evening.

While at the pool, we ran into a couple of my high school friends celebrating a 21st birthday. We took some pictures, had a drink together and parted ways.

Later that evening, all went very smooth and our customer left very satisfied, telling us he wanted to come back before he went home later that week. We said our goodbyes and parted ways, but it was too late to schedule more appointments. So, Serenity and I called it a night and returned to our room to sleep. I called Hans to let him know I was back in the room for the night and he answered right away.

During our conversation, Hans mentioned that he wanted me to get to know Sophia better because she needed more friends. I agreed to be friendly if she wanted to hang out when I got home, but I had no interest in pursuing any further involvement with her. This upset Hans, of course, and he started raising his voice, but I decided to end the call. I had a hard time sleeping that night because I was upset and not feeling very good.

Since I was having a hard time sleeping, I got on social media and saw the pictures we took by the pool with my high school friends. The comments on them shocked me. The boys were being shamed for hiring hookers, and he had to tell them he didn't and that it was me. We were fully dressed, and I didn't think we looked like hookers. Reading the comments cut deep. Had I really lost myself so much that I was unrecognizable?

In the following days, Serenity and I tried to make money in Vegas, but we ended up not achieving what we had hoped. So we made reservations and headed back to the Bay. A few days after returning to Serenity's place, my upset stomach didn't improve, and I felt more tired than usual. Serenity was concerned so she bought me a pregnancy test, which surprisingly came back positive! I wasn't quite sure how to feel.

I decided to wait until I got home to tell Hans, as his family had a tradition for announcing pregnancies. Given that I was on the Depo-Provera shot and always used protection with my clients, I was certain the baby was Hans'.

With the good news to share and a big Halloween party approaching, I cut my trip to the Bay short. I wanted to surprise Hans by showing up unannounced. I headed home to surprise my unsuspecting husband, but he surprised me instead by not being there.

I was told that he had taken Sophia out to eat, which didn't sit well with me, because he hadn't mentioned seeing her that day. I also learned that she had stayed over the night before. My doubts about their relationship were confirmed, but I decided to wait until the two of us could discuss it face-to-face and alone.

When I got home, my roommate offered to take me out for dinner since Hans still hadn't returned. But I was too tired and just wanted to rest. When Hans finally arrived, I was already asleep, too upset to stay awake.

The next day, we went shopping for Halloween costumes and party decorations, trying to stay busy. I never found the right moment to tell Hans about the pregnancy.

While he was at work, I talked to Riley and found out that Sophia had visited our house frequently while I was away. I tried to shake off the feeling of his infidelity because the timing wasn't right. Not only were we throwing a big Halloween party, and our guests would be arriving soon, but the news of my pregnancy still needed to be told.

I had planned to tell Hans about the baby before the guests arrived and had even prepared a cute card for the announcement. While my roommates and I were eating, Hans returned home, and Sophia was with him. He attempted to explain, but I cut him off.

Not wanting to make a scene, I greeted her and excused myself to go change. I knew that hearing about the baby wouldn't be good right now, so I decided to postpone the news until after the party.

As I finished hiding the card I had for Hans, the two of them entered the bedroom. Evidently, Sophia needed a Halloween costume and he had chosen for her a see-through lingerie dress. She complied with his suggestion of the dress, and addressed him as "Sir."

I was fuming inside, and my stomach churned, but once again I swallowed my words, not wanting to argue in front of Sophia. I kept my thoughts to myself for the rest of the night and stayed as far away as I could from the both of them.

I tried not to drink, but it was challenging, especially when they announced a house shot and everyone waited for me to take it. I figured one drink wouldn't hurt, especially since it was early in the pregnancy. However, shortly after taking the shot, a furious Riley had stormed into the garage, confronting Hans for having a girlfriend and making me upset enough to cry. She also warned Sophia to stop her behavior or face consequences.

Riley left, Sophia went inside crying, and Hans stormed over to me, blaming me for the argument and said that I had embarrassed him. The next couple of hours were challenging, and my discomfort persisted.

Soon, I found myself in the bathroom, in excruciating pain. When I saw the blood, that's when I realized I was having a miscarriage. I laid on the cool tile floor and wept, for myself, for my marriage, and for the loss of my baby who I never got to meet.

Feeling completely devastated and broken, I had just learned that my husband was in the next room engaged in intimate activities with Sophia. I was still suffering from the pain of losing the baby, and I had no desire to see or talk to either of them.

I considered staying at friend's or asking one of my roommates if I could sleep on their floor. But before I could make a decision, Hans came out to talk to me. He couldn't understand why I was still upset over the argument.

Furious and frustrated, I decided to tell him everything.

"Hans, I had such sweet news to share with you that I've been trying to tell you for over a week," I retorted. "But with everything you've been doing with Sophia, and how horribly you've treated me, I just couldn't bring myself to tell you. But now it's too late. I was pregnant. We were going to have a baby, but a few hours ago I suffered a miscarriage, and now our baby is gone. I simply wanted Sophia out of our lives in exchange for a more normal one. But I guess that was too much to ask. You're a terrible husband, Hans, and a horrible man. And you probably would have been a dreadful father, too. I'm sorry. I just can't do this right now," I sobbed and walked away.

I was so angry and felt so hurt by everything that had happened. Hans tried to grab my arm as I walked passed him, but I pulled away and went to sleep on the couch. I think he knew better than to try to follow me. Plus, his "faithful subject" was waiting for him in the other room. The one that obeyed, and called him "Sir".

Something was stirring inside of me, but it would be another year before I knew what or Who it was.

21

Not Quite a Happy New Year

The next few weeks at home were uneventful, and Hans and I rarely said much of anything. Before I knew it, I was on my way to Serenity's for another two weeks because the money still wasn't worth going back to the Ranch.

Once I arrived, the two of us enjoyed several appointments and we were both pleased that the money was substantial. Our free time was spent shopping, cooking, and just watching movies together. Soon it was time for me to go home for the holidays. I said my goodbyes and then started my journey back.

It was Wednesday, the day before Thanksgiving, and traffic on the freeway was heavier than normal. About thirty minutes into the drive, a minivan merged into my lane and not having enough room. Thankfully, I had time to react and avoided a head-on collision, but she hit the front side of the car and the back side as well. I was shaken and in pain, but I managed to pull over and call the police. They arrived quickly, filed a report, and suggested I continue driving if I felt good enough since the car wasn't totaled.

After assuring them I was fine, I called Serenity and Devon and they came and checked out the car to verify that it was indeed drivable, so I headed home. I stopped for gas, grabbed an energy drink and a pain reliever in anticipation of the discomfort I'd feel once the shock wore off.

I don't remember much about Thanksgiving because I ended up sleeping on Hans' mom's couch due to the pain pill she had given me.

We celebrated Christmas with Hans' parents and briefly saw my family at my extended family's Christmas gathering. It was uncomfortable given my disappointment regarding their lack of involvement in the wedding, so we didn't stay long to avoid any potential conflicts.

I spent New Year's Eve with Serenity at her apartment. Neither of us felt like going to the club with Devon. Despite having my friend with me, I still felt very much alone, realizing that my focus on making money had taken precedence over spending time with my family during the holidays.

Hans went out with his friends while I received a simple, "Happy New Year, love ya" text instead of a romantic midnight kiss. Our first New Years as husband and wife was far from the image I had hoped for. But I was grateful to be at Serenity's at the beginning of the year as it allowed me to celebrate her birthday with her.

Our plans to go out that weekend were squashed because of an argument between Devon and Serenity about him wanting to work on her birthday. Devon became aggressive, throwing things around the house and yelling. I texted Hans, and he advised us to stay at a hotel for safety. But thankfully, Devon's anger subsided, and he left for the night.

She and I went to the closest fast-food place and ordered takeout. Then we went back to the apartment for a quiet evening just talking and laughing together. The next morning, I went to retrieve something from my car and saw that the driver's side window had been smashed, which I found quite coincidental.

In the end, I decided to cut my trip short and wait until this year's Super Bowl party for me to improve my cash flow.

I still had high hopes that this New Years would be the one that helped me to become someone else, doing something else, before it was too late to do anything else at all.

22

Desperate for Something New

A few days before the Super Bowl party, Hans had agreed to make a birthday cake for one of the wives from his biker group. As soon as I got home, I started baking, because her birthday party happened to fall on the same day as one of his big bike club events. So, he was going to help with the cake decorating, and I would handle the rest.

Just as I finished her cake, my phone rang. It was Hans informing me that he had been in an accident.

"I'm okay," he explained, "I just have some nasty scrapes and bruises, but my bike is totaled." Thankfully, Shane and Riley had a truck, so I didn't need to pick him up. Hans said that I needed to call the insurance company while he was on his way home to report the accident.

When he got home, Shane and Hans unloaded his damaged bike, which was barely recognizable. After I fed him and he showered, he mentioned taking some pain relievers, but insisted we still go to the bar for the birthday party.

I got dressed and ready to go, changing my outfit a couple of times at his suggestion because he always wanted me to look my best and make the other wives jealous. We headed to the bar with the cake and had a fun night drinking and partying.

This year, Destiny asked me to bring a friend, and she planned to bring someone for party entertainment. Serenity accompanied me to the party, but her husband Devon was not invited, and she agreed to those terms.

A few days later, we both worked the Super Bowl party and the money we both made was amazing. The only difference was that this year's party was held at one of the guys' houses with a more selective group of attendees. The two of us made more money than in previous years, which was the financial boost we needed.

Every year, this event served as my annual financial boost, similar to what most people experience with their tax returns. During the party, it was apparent that Cory and Destiny were facing serious marital issues, which began to affect Hans and my relationship with them.

Despite only shooting a scene or two in the past few months, I decided to join Destiny at the AVN Convention. My intention was to enjoy the show, maybe walk the convention floor, and provide her with some company.

Just before I left to meet her at her house, she called in a panic and told me that Cory had become violent again, but this time it was even more severe. It was the straw breaking the camel's back, and she finally had enough.

Destiny asked me to meet her at her apartment in Los Angeles because she was leaving Cory for good. Her plan was to move out while he was at his softball game, because she didn't know how he would react if he knew she was really leaving. So, instead of going to the convention, Hans and I drove down to make sure she was okay.

Shortly after we arrived at her place, Cory and his daughter showed up, and asked to talk to her, but Hans insisted that they wait until he calmed down. It turned into a late night with me comforting his daughter while Hans mediated their conversation.

Tensions grew over the next few months between Cory and Hans, and in order to prevent additional drama, it lead us to avoid family functions where Cory might show up.

Their divorce made me reflect on how the industry had started to strain our relationship, and I desperately began to desire a normal job that would allow me to be home with my husband.

I decided I would do whatever it took to exit the industry. However, when I expressed my feelings to Hans, he shared concerns about our financial situation, and then he insisted that I not quit my job until further notice from him. So, of course, I obeyed. It was how I was programed.

The next few months, I continued alternating between trips to the Ranch and visiting Serenity's place, with each trip taking a greater toll on me than the last. Even my roommates started noticing, and began asking me not to go because they could see the distress on my face every time I packed my bags.

I knew time for me was running out, and I could not wait for Hans' approval any longer. I decided on my own that this would be my last summer at the Ranch, and I began to seriously search for new ways to make money.

I also believed it was time to close off our marriage to others because I knew deep down that, as a married couple, we shouldn't be involved with other people outside the marriage. Unfortunately for me, Hans did not agree, and I suffered through several more difficult months and scoldings.

23

No Such Thing as Normal

I desperately wanted for Hans and I to have a normal life, and over the next few months, I found myself becoming the maternal figure in the house. I was the one cooking dinner even though I wasn't very good at it. I even messed up a dinner out of a box, and then sat on the hood of my car crying because I knew my future children were going to starve to death. Either that or we would live off McDonald's because of my inability in the kitchen.

I was the one who would deep clean the house whenever I had a chance, the one who walked the dogs and, if someone got sick, I'd hover over them until I knew they would be okay.

When our newest roommate found out she was a few months pregnant, I felt obligated to make sure she was doing what she needed to do to have a healthy pregnancy, and to ensure she had all the sleep necessary. Everyone started calling me "Mom" after I forced Derrick, who was trying to live off frozen hot Cheetos, energy drinks and beer, to sit down and eat a heathy breakfast that I managed to put together.

Hans and I started making and selling specialty cakes as a side hustle, and I started applying for other work while we saved up whatever we could.

Soon it was time to celebrate Hans' birthday, and I always threw a big party for him. Our house was a party house more often than not, but for this party I spent double what I normally would, and I made a cake and nice dinner for us and our roommates before people came over. Not only was I the maternal figure as of late, but the domestic one as well.

Since I was being so accommodating lately, Hans chose to approach me in the middle of his party, informing me that for his birthday he wanted me and my friend Christine to take care of his needs. I was appalled. How dare he use his birthday to make me feel obligated to change my mind about opening up our marriage in order to satisfy his sick desires.

Once again, Hans reminded me when we first got together, that I had agreed to be in an open relationship if I wanted to have a relationship with him, and it was never going to change! Not even now that we were married!

So several drinks later, here we were again sharing our

bedroom with a third person. My husband said it wasn't going to be anything but some foreplay involving her, yet again, that was a lie. How was I supposed to close our marriage and keep our bedroom private when he could charm any girl into doing anything he asked?

If Hans and I were to stay together, it would be a very long time before he and I would ever live as a happily married couple sharing a sacred bedroom together as one. He never wanted to and he never would... and because of this my heart ached for someone normal.

In July, after applying for what felt like a million different positions over the next few weeks, I finally caught a break and was offered a chance to have a normal job being a bar back. (A bar back is someone who assists the bartender so they can concentrate on their customers.) I made one last trip to the Ranch to collect my things, and to make some quick cash before I started my new job.

I took advantage of this being my last trip and spent most of my free time with my family who lived nearby since I wasn't sure when I would be seeing them again.

Things were going fairly well considering, and us girls even had done some filming for the HBO show and threw a big pool party just for the crew during this trip. I had one last "double girl" appointment as a last hoorah for us both to make some good money before heading home.

When I called Hans after the appointment to let him know I

was finished and going to bed, he informed me that the Scion had been repossessed again. Hans also told me how proud he was when he purposedly tried to scare the guy as he was loading the car onto the tow truck. That's when Hans came walking outside covered in tattoos and holding our Pitbull in an attempt to deter the guy from taking the car. It didn't work, and Hans ended up just handing over the keys. Now he wanted me to call them and pay the fees to get the car back.

I called the finance company, and they told me my payment was late, and that if a car had been repossessed once, and if you fall behind even one month that they could take the car. I was so tired of Hans not contributing enough to keep his payments on time, and I told them to just keep the car! After all, he still had the newly repaired motorcycle.

I went to bed not feeling the least bit guilty, and was able to get some sleep before heading home to what I hoped would be my new and improved life.

In the beginning, everything was going fairly well, even though money was a little tighter than we had hoped. But after a few weeks, I started to make some good tips. I was even able to pay for another tattoo, but this time I broke the unwritten tattoo rule and had our initials put on my wrist; even after everyone, including the artist told me it was a jinx. I was smart enough to have him design it to where if I needed to, I could cover up the letters.

Since I was now officially no longer part of the "industry", my mom invited Hans and I to go with them to the local amusement park and try to mend our relationship. We met them there and spent the day with them, riding the rides and trying to have fun. Unfortunately, it felt very awkward, and I could tell that my family still disliked Hans very much, but they were trying hard to get through the day.

Of course, my mom hated the tattoo, but liked the fact that I had a backup plan just in case. After a long day of trying to keep the peace and enjoy ourselves as if there was no weird disconnect between us, it was finally time to go home.

On the way back in the car, Hans said, "Amanda, you should reward me for dealing with your family all day!" Then he insisted that I take care of him right then! I didn't want to, and I asked him nicely if he could please wait until we got home. But Hans being Hans gave me that look and told me, "You can either do it now, or you can deal with the punishment when we get home. Your choice!"

My heart was pounding hard, but I stood my ground. I figured it would be better to take his punishment than to be in a compromising position when we were pulled over since it was still daylight outside. He pouted and fumed, and I had nothing to say, so we drove home in silence.

When we got home, no one was there. Our roommate had gone to pick up his daughter, and the house was empty. My heart started racing. As soon as Hans realized the house was empty, he knew he was going to take full advantage of it.

I was headed down the hall towards our bedroom when my husband grabbed me and pushed me against the wall, holding me by the throat and telling me it was time for my punishment. What he did to me after that an animal didn't deserve.

I was choking and gagging as my tears and makeup covered my face. Then he forced me down to my knees telling me how much he loved seeing my makeup run down my face. After a while, he stopped and pulled me up off the floor. Then he told me to go into the bedroom. When we got there, I was told to strip and get on my hands and knees while he decided the rest of my punishment!

Soon he began whipping me with a belt or coat hanger (which ever was handy), and hitting me as hard as he could, making sure I cried out in pain. He continued to tell me how sexy I looked with my makeup smeared all over, and when he felt I had had enough, he told me to drop down in front of him and he would finish himself off. His brutality seemed to get worse with every punishment, and it would take days, sometimes weeks for my bruised body to heal.

24

Fun & Games, Until it Wasn't

I quickly realized that only working at the bar wasn't going to be enough money to keep me from the sex industry, and I was desperate not to go back. So I applied at a few seasonal places in September. Hans was hired by a local seasonal Halloween store as a manager since he had been working for their sister company for a while, and we thought it would be a good idea for me to work there as well. I knew the Halloween store would be a temporary position, so I contiued to apply at other places and was hired for a second seasonal position at one of the local craft stores.

With Hans now working full time and me balancing all three jobs, life was really busy, but at least I was able to keep from going back to the Ranch like I was so desperate not to do. Luckily, I had the same uniform at two of the jobs, so it made switching from one to the other much easier. I mostly ate my meals while driving to the next job, and tried to catch naps in between shifts if needed.

The next few weeks flew by, and it was time to celebrate Halloween again. I'm still not totally sure why this holiday was so important for us to celebrate. Maybe it was because I never was allowed to celebrate as a kid. It was Satan's day and my folks refused to acknowledge him. I had forgotten this since being with Hans, so every year we both felt the need to make it fun.

However, this year I wouldn't be able to join the boys and throw a party at the house because I had to work at the bar. To this day, I still don't know how the party at the house went; only that I had to clean up the horrendous mess when I got home. It was also a busy night at the bar, and all the weirdos in their costumes were running wild.

I had finally worked my way from a bar back position to a full-time bartender, and Halloween was one of my first really busy nights. It was a night full of specialty drinks, costume contests, and karaoke, and it was definitely interesting.

When I got home, my very drunk husband was already in bed sleeping, and I figured I would just crawl under the covers quietly as to not disturb him, but that was not the case. The dogs were excited to see me, and they ended up waking him up.

I had hoped to just say good night and go to sleep, but as soon as I laid down, Hans started kissing my neck and telling me about some "hot girl" who was at the party and how turned on he was, and that I needed to take care of him now.

"Please, Hans, I just can't. I am really tried," I tried telling him, but he wasn't listening.

The next thing I know, he's pulling my head back by my hair and putting his hand around my throat, choking me, and yelling, "I am the Master! You are my slave. Don't you ever forget it!

I went along with his perverted antics so that it would be over soon, and I could sleep. But apparently, I hadn't move fast enough. His raised his hand in the air, and it came down hard across my face. Then he told me to get a move on. I finally gave in and did what he wanted. Luckily for me, it didn't take long for him to finish. I waited until I heard him snoring and knew he was passed out before I could relax and fall asleep. The next morning, he acted like nothing happened, as he greeted me with a kiss on the cheek.

Nights continued to be busy at the bar and the days at the house always seemed to be overcrowded with roommates and their guests just hanging around. This was when I realized that this wasn't the kind of house I wanted to raise a family in. So once again, we started looking for a new place, and we felt we could do it without having to have any roommates.

After a short search, we found the perfect house across town to rent. I was so excited about a big two-story house with a garage, a yard for the dogs, and the best part was it was only two doors down from my best friend and her husband. Things really seemed to be settling down and lining up for us to have a family, and what I thought would be a normal life.

Hans was still at the party store, and we continued to make cakes on the side just because we enjoyed making them. I was able to quit my part-time jobs because I got a raise at the bar, and was working a lot more hours. I also started to have some regular repeat customers.

One guy that came in often, always joked with me, asking me when I was going to get a divorce so that I could marry him. It was fun bantering back and forth for a while. Then one night in late December, he came in acting a little strange. He looked like maybe he was on something and not just drunk. His eyes had this weird, dilated look, and he was more physical, wanting to hug on me instead of our usual hello and goodbye hug. There was even a time that he tried to follow me behind the bar. That's when I asked my manager to have him leave. But then after they talked things seemed to calm down, so we let him stay.

Later in the night, a glass was dropped and broke just on the other side of the bar, and I bent down to clean it up. When I stood up, I felt an arm wrap around me from behind like someone was going to give me a hug. But the next thing I knew, the arm wrapped around my neck and I was in a chokehold, and was having a hard time breathing.

Thankfully, one of my female customers caught on to what was happening, and she helped me get out of the chokehold. When I turned around, I noticed that it was the same guy who would sit at my bar. I rushed back behind the bar to the backroom to collect my thoughts when someone tried to open the door. Thinking it was him again, I stood still and didn't make a sound.

Then there was another knock, and I heard a female voice calling my name. It was that same customer asking if I was okay, and I told her I was just a little shaken and was going to go to the bathroom to wash my face. I headed to the bathroom, and I heard her yell at a guy to back off, and when I came out, she said he had tried to follow me.

After an hour, I was hot and needed some air, so I went outside in the back. The next thing I knew the same guy had me against the wall next to the door with his hand on my throat. I starting kicking him and trying to yell to tell him to stop.

As he leaned in to kiss me, the bar manager walked out the door looking for me and he grabbed him by the shoulder and told him to get lost. I was shaken, and I wanted to go home but it was a busy Saturday night and we needed both bartenders, so I stuck it out. I stayed behind the bar and had the manager and bouncer walk me to my car when I got off work.

When I got home, I went straight to bed without telling Hans anything because I didn't think he would let it go, and I didn't want him messing with this guy since I knew the guy was hanging around gang members.

When I came back to work after having two days off, I sat down with the owners and told them what had happened and informed them I wanted to have a bouncer on the weeknights that I worked even though there normally wasn't one.

They proceeded to watch the cameras and told me they couldn't see anything wrong from what they could tell and said they couldn't afford a bouncer on weekdays. I told them I was worried about my safety, and they said they would inform the guy he wasn't allowed to come back, but it was a "No" for the additional staff during the week.

The next night I was talking to one of my regulars about it and she told me it was time to find another job and that the restaurant and bar she cooked at was looking for a new bartender. She said if I wanted her to, she would talk to them about me. She and her friends were going to go to another bar, but she said she would text her boss and come back by.

A few hours later they came back, and not only did she tell me to come in the next day for an interview, but that they had found out from the bartender downtown that the same guy I had problems with had shot his gun at the ceiling in a downtown bar a few nights ago. That was enough for me to decide to go for the interview and get away from him before it was a problem.

A few days later I had my interview and was hired on the spot. I let the other bar manager know that I didn't feel safe and was taking another job, and I thanked them for teaching me all they had since I had come into that bar without any training.

I gave them my two-week's notice and did my two weeks without incident. Then I went off to the new bar that sat on the waters of the California Delta.

25

The Start of New Beginnings

Starting a new year at a new bar made me feel like this was my chance to have a brand-new fresh start. No one knew who I was or what my past looked like. My duties would not only consist of being a bartender, but also a waitress since the main waitress had to have foot surgery.

I was grateful to be working at just one place, instead of three, and able to do specialty cakes on the side for fun, instead of necessity. Not only did I start the year with a new job, but we had moved into the new house, too. It truly seemed like this would finally be the fresh start to a new life that I had been asking for and dreaming about for so long.

I quickly became close to the girls I worked with, and it felt as if this would be the safest bar to be working. The only issue Hans and I had at the time had nothing to do with work. It was our poor dog Charlie who had been gaining an unusual amount of weight and getting oddly lazy.

When we took him to the vet, we found out that he was suffering from thyroid issues and would have to be on medication for the rest of his life. Poor Charlie.

Since I was working a lot of hours, we needed a second vehicle that wasn't a motorcycle. Luckily, we found an older Chevy Silverado truck for $1500 and bought it. Now that Hans had a truck, he decided to start a handyman business on the side in hopes to one day leave the party supply store.

I ordered business cards for him and started advertising his company on social media. I did whatever I could to help him be successful, but it never took off. As time went on, I realized that with Hans slowly working his way out of the party store trying to run a business over those few months, we ended up behind on bills again and having a hard time affording the dog's medicine.

I was so tired of struggling financially and wondering where the next dollar would come from, so I decided we should probably search for another roommate, and the sooner the better.

One night I was sharing with my foster brother about our dilemma, and before I knew it, I was offering him and his girlfriend our extra room upstairs. They too were struggling so I looked at it as a win, win for us all.

My brother loved me, and I knew he wouldn't skip out on his bills or his obligations. He was also a hard worker, so he and his girlfriend moved in, and for a while thing were going smoothly.

The four of us would take turns making dinner, and everyone chipped in and cleaned up. Of course, my brother didn't mind at all being my taste tester when it came to making cakes, which was much more successful than the handyman business.

Thanks to a few coworkers who placed orders, we were able to make larger, more elaborate cakes, and with a few extra hundred dollars, I'd be able to give Hans another nice birthday party in March, as well. This time it was just our friends and his family having drinks and playing games.

Since my brother was now living with us, I told Hans we could no longer have an open relationship going on behind closed doors, and that I wanted to close the marriage again. Of course, Hans wasn't happy about it, but he seemed to understand that I didn't want my brother to see any of that, so he kept things to a minimum.

One night while my brother and his girlfriend were away from the house, we had a small group of friends over for a house party. I went upstairs to give Charlie his medicine, and not too soon after, the talking downstairs became louder and had gotten very rowdy. They sounded like they were having fun, and I wanted to join them. But when I got the bottom of the stairs, it became blatantly obvious why they were being too loud. While I was upstairs tending to Charlie and without my knowledge, Hans had put in one of my "movies" because he wanted to show off to our friends what I could do.

When I walked in the room, I was mortified and so embarrassed, and I started crying. Through my tears, I scolded Hans, "Turn that off or I'm leaving," I yelled, and I walked into the kitchen.

The room got really quiet, so I figured they had shut it off, but I was wrong. All they had done was turn the sound off and continued to watch. They could not take their eyes off the screen. I was so upset, and I left in tears.

How dare he do that to me! What was he thinking? What I hoped would remain my secret, at least for a little while, was a secret no more. They all knew now that I had been a porn star, but what I couldn't understand was why they had to watch it in my house with me there!

By the time I got back home, everyone had gone, and Hans was cleaning up. When he saw me, he said, "I'm sorry, Mandie. I didn't see the harm. I'm proud of who you were, and what you were, and you were good at it too! But I shouldn't have exposed you without asking you first. Forgive me," he asked, and he almost sounded sincere.

Of course, I forgave him, because that's how I was programmed, and that was the last of anyone bringing it up, at least in front of me. Soon, it felt as if we were moving past the days of the "industry" and opened marriage romps. In fact, it was the closest we had ever gotten to what most people would call a normal relationship.

Since I was out of the "industry" my family welcomed me back in their lives as my baby sister was getting married soon. I felt like part of the family again when they invited me to help pick out her wedding dress, and then join them for lunch afterwards.

I really thought things were changing for the better and going back to how it used to be. But that time helping with the wedding dress was the last time I was asked to be a part of the wedding, until the family photos a few hours prior to my sister's big day. She later told me she was worried I would do something to make it about me and not her, or try to sabotage her day.

The ceremony was beautiful, and they were lucky enough to even have a little butterfly join them. I had heard once that butterflies were supposed to be a sign of peace and calm, and something special from above. So when I saw it flutter past them, it felt as if they had been blessed.

After dinner, my Papa needed to go to the hotel to rest, and we didn't want my Gran to miss out on the wedding, so Hans helped him back to the hotel.

I couldn't bring myself to watch the first dance with the bride and groom, because my dad hadn't been there for me at mine, and it still hurt, even after all this time. I didn't watch them cut their cake or throw the bouquet either because I was just too emotional.

Towards the end of the night, my cousin, Jeremiah, came over to check on me. He and I had always been really close, and he was able to talk me into going out on the dance floor with him, and having some fun. I finally gave in and I'm glad I did. I really did have a great time dancing the rest of the night, and eventually Hans and I headed home.

Life carried on over the next few weeks with me working full time, us making cakes on the side and spending time with friends. Hans started to do a lot more with the motorcycle club, so that was starting to fill up any free time we had.

I got a random Saturday night off and we went out with the club and ended up needing a right home. Luckily Riley's son Miguel was able to come save the day. Miguel stayed the night at our house since it was so late. Hans joked with me saying, "I bet you regret wanting to close the marriage now," because he knew I found Miguel attractive and now I couldn't have him.

The next morning, Miguel was already gone so I sent him a thank you text message, which led to us texting a lot over the next few weeks. I found myself so comfortable with him that I even opened up about my past and how I was struggling to get Hans to have a closed marriage. It was so nice to have someone to confide in that wasn't expecting anything in return.

A few months later, we found out that I was pregnant again. I was over the moon elated, and surprisingly, Hans seemed to be excited too. That was when we both agreed to "close" the marriage for good, so we could focus on our growing family.

With money getting tighter and a growing family, we started looking for ways to cut our expenses and living a cleaner more productive life. I was doing my best to work extra shifts, but the summer weather had gone away rather abruptly, and the bar was slow. My cash tips had almost dwindled down to nothing.

Not to mention being pregnant and working at a restaurant that served seafood was miserable for me. It was difficult to bring food out of the kitchen without the seafood smell kicking my nausea into high gear.

The staff had done their best to assist me in bringing out the food and also helping me with the heavy lifting. The head chef knew I had suffered a miscarriage in the past, and he would do everything he could to make my job easier. I was very lucky to have such wonderfully caring bosses and co-workers.

26

‿⁓‿

A Baby Won't Fix It

With tips at a minimum and money not coming in, my husband and I faced another housing crisis. We needed to find a more affordable place to live. Luckily for us, a friend offered to let us rent a single-wide trailer on his property for $600 a month, cutting our rent in half.

Despite my initial sadness about leaving our beautiful house, Hans promised to transform the trailer into a comfortable home. We cleaned and painted to make it our own. Though it wasn't a permanent arrangement, we still made the best of it, even as I wondered how I would navigate the tight hallways with my growing belly.

Deep down I felt like I was sinking to a new low. I hated the idea of raising my child in the trailer with no heat and barely enough hot water, but again it was going to be a temporary thing, so I went along with it.

We decided it was time to share our pregnancy news with close friends and family. Hans followed his family tradition of gifting a binky to his parents, who were thrilled by our news. We surprised my parents at the restaurant where I worked, but our attempt at humor with a binky in my dad's beer didn't quite go as planned. Nonetheless, they were happy for us. I took it as a sign that they were finally warming up to Hans.

At my request, my mom and sister came with me to my first doctor's appointment, which unfortunately turned into an argument about genetic testing. It was an embarrassing moment, and I couldn't wait to leave. The doctor postponed the ultrasound for a few days due to a malfunction on the machine.

One night, just before my shift had ended, Hans called me from his friends' house, and said, "I'm still here at the party, but a fight just broke out and it's getting pretty ugly. You need to come and pick me up when you get off." It was more of a command than a request.

By the time I got there, another altercation had occurred. So, me being the fixer that I was, I tried calming one of the men down, and found myself in the middle of their fight. In the chaos, I ended up getting thrown into a large Snap-on toolbox and hurting my stomach. Later that night, I started cramping, but I didn't see any blood, so I didn't rush to the emergency room, and instead, I just rested at home.

On the day of my rescheduled ultrasound, Hans was working on his bike and said he couldn't take me, so Riley said she would come with me. When we got to the hospital, the technician said that she wasn't allowed to tell us anything because she was not a doctor. I didn't think anything of it, and I didn't know what I would ask her anyway. She did the ultrasound, and I thought I saw the heartbeat, but she wasn't willing to confirm that for me. When I looked over at Riley, she seemed to be very focused on the screen.

After the technician was through, she said the doctor would call me and go over all my results at my next appointment. I was able to get another appointment, but I had a feeling that I shouldn't go alone after a usually talkative Riley just quickly hugged me and rushed off to her car.

Hans couldn't come with me due to prior plans, so I went alone. I sat in his office and waited, scared and anxious. When he came in, I knew his news wasn't good.

The doctor apologized as he informed me that my baby measured only nine weeks instead of twelve, and that there was no heartbeat. I had lost my baby. I was devastated. He couldn't give me a reason, only that it was not uncommon.

I opted for a D&C surgery instead of taking the pills that forced my body into aborting the baby. The doctor made the appointment and told me how sorry he was. Then I drove home, and I wept all the way.

Telling Hans about the loss was heart-wrenching, and the following days were somber. I asked my mom if she would accompany me to the surgery, but she couldn't make it. Hans' mom went with me, though she seemed rushed and distant. The nurse was kind, but I felt alone. It was the saddest day of my life.

After surgery, Hans wanted me to stay in the hospital longer, but I insisted on going home. I was adamant when I said, "If I'm going to lay in a bed and be miserable and depressed, I want to do it in my own bed." It was smart of Hans not to argue.

His aunt unexpectedly came to help, as she was worried that Hans wouldn't be able to provide me with the care I needed emotionally, and she was right. She truly cared, and I felt loved when my brother and his girlfriend came by and shared in my grief.

I reached out to my friend Mia, who was getting married that weekend, but because of my condition, I wouldn't be able to attend. Mia insisted that I stay home, and my attempts to go to the wedding were thwarted, which seemed to just add to my grief.

I really wanted to take it easy, but by day three I couldn't handle looking at the dirty pawprints on the tile anymore. So I filled a bucket with water and grabbed the mop. In my attempt to clean the living room floor, I ended up bleeding heavily and had to sit down. My friend Lucas came to the rescue and helped me clean up. He was there to take care of me.

Although my family didn't seem to be 100 percent accepting of me with Hans yet, I was so very grateful to my friends who were always there for me, and always willing to lend a hand. I could not begin to thank them enough.

27

Shame on Me, Shame on You

Weeks had passed and the crushing pain from the loss of my child was buried deep inside my heart. It was time for me to get up, go back to work and start living again.

The first thing we did was go to a Halloween party... big surprise! This year we didn't host but attended the motorcycle club's party with Shane and Riley. I had a great time letting loose with the girls, drinking and dancing the night away. It was a much-needed escape from the loss of the baby.

At some point, Hans called me over and told me to flash one of the guys. I laughed and told him no, and headed back to the girls thinking nothing of it.

On the way home, we stopped to get some fast food. As were

leaving the drive thru, I was telling him about some of the fun with the girls, and my story was cut abruptly by Hans grabbing me by the throat and slamming me against the seat. Then he told me if I ever embarrassed him in front of his friends again by telling him no, there would be severe punishments. Then he let go and we drove home in silence, and he acted as if he had done nothing wrong.

Life seemed fairly normal for a few weeks, until one night when we were having dinner with some close friends, Michael and Emma, and Hans suggested that we do a wife swap. The two of them had never been with anyone else, and the wife seemed overly curious and very eager to see if she and her husband should try for an open marriage.

I truly did not want to start this up again. I thought it was behind us and that we had moved on and "closed" our marriage for good. But I was mistaken, again. How many times can one person be so wrong about the person they were married to? God only knows.

Hans just couldn't let it go. He was a sick man, and I was so tired of this life. However, with Hans' pitiful begging and pleading, and Emma's curiosity, I begrudgingly gave in, for I was still that person who had been programed to say "Yes" so long ago. Was this my doom? Would I ever be normal. Would my marriage?

That following weekend Emma and I swapped places. She came

over to the trailer, and I went over to her house. After Michael put their toddler to bed, we sat on the couch and watched a movie to see where this would go. I was spending the night so there was no need to rush into anything.

It was a bit strange snuggling on the couch with someone else's husband, but I trusted Michael, and I could tell he was just as nervous as me. He suggested we have a drink to relax, and I happily agreed. After we finished, I figured if this thing was going to happen, I would have to be the one to initiate it.

I leaned in and started kissing his neck and running my hand on his leg. Of course, this got things going, but he said he didn't want to risk waking up the baby so we should go to the bedroom. That's when he scooped me up and carried me to their room.

The rest happened behind closed doors, and it wasn't horrible. Michael was kind and gentle, nothing like Hans who was uncaring and rough, and only focused on himself.

I decided it would be best if I slept on the couch just in case their son woke up, and Michael agreed. We didn't want to confuse the little guy, and I didn't mind sleeping on the couch at all. The next morning, he made me pancakes, then we loaded up his little boy and headed to the trailer.

On the way over, we talked in very brief detail about the previous night's events, and both of us said that it was a nice time, but we didn't want it to happen again, because we didn't want to ruin our friendship.

After Michael went home, I asked Hans about his night, and he raved about it. He went on and on telling me how naturally submissive Emma was. Then I told him about me and Michael, and thought this would probably be a "one-time only" thing and Hans just laughed, saying, "We'll see."

It was still slow at the bar and cold outside, so I found myself goofing around with coworkers more than waiting on customers because there really wasn't much foot traffic. I had become very close with one of the chefs, and I told her how unhappy I was with my marriage, and how I wanted to leave Hans, but I just couldn't bring myself to do it.

I had started texting my friend Miguel (Riley's oldest son) a while back when Hans decided he wanted the marriage open again, and Miguel let me vent. . . again. He was always so patient and kind, and I knew what we had was a very special friendship. Miguel respected that I was a married woman, and he would not cross the line, and I respected him for respecting me.

One morning after Hans had gone to work, Miguel stopped by to see how I was doing. I was an emotional wreck and could not stop crying. Miguel put his arms around me and allowed me to cry until I was all cried out. Snot and tears were all over his shirt, but he didn't seem to mind.

Before he left, he gave me a kiss on the cheek and whispered, "You know I'm in love with you, right?" I teared up again, and said, "I can't say it back, Miguel, because I'm married." But I knew that he knew I felt the same. With that, he went home and the both of us went back to just texting randomly every now and then.

It was New Year's Eve and a busy night for all the bars around the city. And I was stuck at mine. I had to work while my friends went out. At least, I wasn't the closing bartender, so I was able to meet up with everyone after my shift ended and be the designated driver if it was needed. And not to my surprise, it was needed.

My friend Erica ended up staying the night at the trailer with us since she had carpooled with Hans to meet everyone else. I was so tired from working all day and just wanted to go to bed, but Hans and Erica had other plans. They had had enough to drink while they were out, and they decided we should ring in the New Year with a three way.

Oh dear, please not again! But I knew there would be repercussions, and I would be punished severely if I didn't comply. So I went along with it briefly, but then I saw an opportunity for escape. I left to get a glass of water, and they continued without me. I don't even think they noticed I was gone.

I had no desire to actually be a part of it, so I just let the two of them finish up together, and I waited on the couch watching tv and texting Miguel until they passed out. Then I went to bed alone.

28

Nearing the End

Here we were a few days into the new year, celebrating my sister and her new husband. My middle sister and her fiancé decided to get married in early January in Reno. So, Hans and I packed our bags along with my bridesmaid dress and headed to my aunt's to help her make their wedding cake.

On the way over the hill, Hans and I got into an argument, and we couldn't seem to resolve anything. While we were working on the cake, neither one of us could let it go, and Hans decided to spend the night at my aunt's instead of my Gran's, as we had originally planned.

I left to go to my Gran's without my husband and spent the

rest of the night telling her that we had been having serious disagreements lately, and things weren't going well at home. I confided in her because I didn't want my parents to know, fearing they would say, "I told you so." Gran was always someone I could trust to keep my private stuff private.

Early the next morning, Gran and I headed to the wedding venue with our hair and makeup ready so we could assist where they needed assistance. Thankfully, my sister had a hair and makeup coordinator, so we didn't have to do much except to get dressed.

I mostly stayed with the wedding party and only saw Hans briefly when they set up the cake and the DJ booth. I was still upset that he didn't come with me the night before. He made it clear that he had no interest in being around my family except for my aunt and uncle. He spent the day with my uncle, avoiding my entire family.

Besides the family pictures that we were required to be in, the two of us spent most of the day keeping our distance. It must have been pretty obvious because I was questioned a few times throughout the day.

Instead of engaging in uncomfortable conversations with any of them, I answered their questions briefly and changed the subject. Before I knew it, it was time to leave, and we headed back home to California. The silence in the car was deafening.

The next couple of weeks were uneventful and the house was quiet. The bar was still slow, and I was glad we had moved into the trailer and not having to pay a lot of money for rent. Hans occasionally worked with our landlord's son learning how to be a trucker, but it wasn't steady income, so we relied on my bartending and tips to get by. Hans was spending more time with our friends than he was at home while I was working late shifts.

A short time later, Hans and Emma pushed for one more night together, but Michael and I were not interested. We reluctantly agreed to let her visit my house while I went to theirs, but both myself and Michael had no intention of engaging in any more intimate rendezvous. We felt things would become awkward if we continued with these arrangements, so we decided to go out to dinner and watch a movie instead.

Hans and Emma's relationship had escalated to a level that Michael and I were not comfortable with. We wanted them to stop, and I shared this several times to Hans. He wasn't happy with the idea because he wanted someone who would fully submit to him and do whatever he wanted, and Emma evidently jumped through hoops for him.

However, because it bothered me, Hans told me he would talk to Emma, leading both Michael and me to believe that they would stop since our original agreement had been, "If anyone felt uncomfortable, we would cease these arrangements."

That afternoon, Emma received a call which allowed her to leave work early. Instead of staying home with her husband, she came over to our house while I was at work, and she and Hans were once again intimate. I received several messages from Hans as he bragged to me about it, and I was very upset.

I called Hans on my break and insisted that he and Emma stop. He promised that this time would be their last time, but he lied again. When I got home, Hans admitted that Emma had come back to our house on the same day, and they once again engaged in another intimate session. Why does he even bother telling me? It's like he's proud of all his sick shenanigans and enjoyed rubbing it in my face.

That weekend, I went out with some of the girls to a club downtown. It was a nice break from the stuff that had been going on inside my house, and I wanted to put it out of my mind.

The next week was better as things had calmed down and returned to some kind of normal. The texting between Hans and Emma had slowed down, and I kept my conversations with Miguel at a minimal.

As a late Valentine's Day gift, Hans and Emma convinced Michael and me to let them have one last intimate session. At this point, I honestly didn't care anymore because I had accepted that this was the state of my marriage, unless I chose to leave.

While the two of them were together, Michael and I took his

son out for root beer floats, and I confessed to him that I didn't know how to make them stop wanting to be together. We both agreed that he would have a talk with his wife and make it clear to her that this would be the absolute last time she and Hans would have together, or there would be consequences.

Two days later Hans had to work, and I decided to go shopping. On my way, I stopped by Miguel's to talk to him. It had been awhile, and I wanted him to know what was going on.

In our conversation, I admitted to him how much I cared for him but, "I really don't know what to do. I want to be with you, but until Hans and I can come to some sort of an agreement, I don't know how to leave him."

Miguel was so sweet and sympathetic, and he tried his best to encourage me, but it was no use. As I explained to him, "I also don't want to be ridiculed by my family for giving up on my marriage or hearing about how I could have avoided it all together had I just listened to them in the first place, and never married Hans."

We talked for a while longer, and he promised, "Amanda, I'll wait as long as it takes for you to figure things out. I'm not going anywhere." Once again, he kissed me on my cheek and squeezed my hand gently to reassure me that he meant what he said.

On my way home, I stopped by Riley's and talked to her about everything. I think she knew deep down that her son had feelings for me. She continued to encourage me because she was afraid for me, and she gave me some great advice.

"Don't worry about other people's opinion, Amanda," she said. "I have had great concerns about your marriage because I saw a lot of similarities that you were going through, which I, too, had gone through in my first marriage. My advice to you is to get out while you can before he loses control and ends up hurting you, like my ex did to me, and it was bad. Please, Amanda, get out!"

As I drove the rest of the way home, I thought about what Riley had shared, and I knew she was right. I had been programed for so long to say Yes. I needed to be reprogrammed and learn how to say, "No. It's not okay. It's over, and I'm done."

29

From Bad to Worse

That night while I was at work, my phone kept ringing, but I was busy and couldn't answer it. I had several missed calls and texts from Hans, Riley, Emma, Michael, and Miguel.

I called Riley back first, and she informed me that Hans had called, upset about something and that it wasn't safe to go home. She offered to let me stay at her place if I needed. I also sent a text to Miguel, saying I would call him after I talked to Hans to find out what was going on. Miguel had a similar story to Riley's. I was so confused; I didn't know what had caused the conflict between the boys.

I decided to call Hans when I had a break. He answered the

phone, and he was angry, insisting that I come home because he wanted to talk. Apparently, Hans had heard some things that I confided to Emma about at our girls' nights. I told him I couldn't deal with this while I was at work and that we would talk after my shift.

Later that night when I walked into the trailer, Hans was waiting on the couch with an almost empty bottle of whiskey. He started accusing me of cheating, and I just sat there, listening to him. It was very confusing to be with a person like this. How does one determine "cheating" when our entire life together was built around infidelity and sexual immorality?

Evidently Hans was upset because he found out that Miguel had feelings for me, and that I was curious about exploring them. I started crying and apologized for hurting him. He seemed deeply hurt, and I genuinely felt bad. I told him I didn't want to end our marriage and asked how I could fix things.

He told me, "Delete Miguel's number from your phone and then get undressed and go to the bedroom," as he believed that his perverted sex was the only way to fix our marriage. I didn't want to argue with him, especially since he had been drinking, so I went along with it.

After some horribly physical confrontation, he demanded that I tell him a particular explicit story, which made me uncomfortable due to my past traumas. When I objected, he became aggressive and hit me. He then threatened to record it and forced me to comply. I just wanted it to end, fearing what might happen if I resisted further.

Afterward, he told me to cuddle with him, and I was left feeling confused and overwhelmed, unsure of how to process what had happened. When I laid down beside him, I started to cry and he grabbed my throat from behind. Before he finally let me go, he pulled my head back by my hair and kissed me. He then told me, "Good night." Then he rolled over and passed out.

The next morning, Hans found that Miguel was still on my Facebook page and became even more enraged. I deleted Miguel, but I also noticed some strange text messages on my phone that were marked as read. Hans had gone through my entire phone looking for evidence against me.

I had gotten a text from my mom, who asked me to meet her for lunch, sensing that something was wrong. I briefly explained the situation to her and agreed to meet.

At lunch, I shared a simplified version with my parents of the open marriage Hans had insisted we have. My mom couldn't hide her shock at what Hans had done and her expression showed how concerned she was. She suggested I spend the night at their place to clear my head before making any decisions.

Hans kept texting and calling me, but I decided to stay with my parents for the night. It was safer, especially since he had been drinking and taking pills, and threatening to kill himself. It was another control tactic, and I wasn't going to fall for it again.

The next morning, my mom said she had nightmares about me returning to the trailer, and insisted that I not go back alone. She made a call to my aunt in Nevada and arranged for me to stay with her. They wanted me to be far away from whatever Hans had up his sleeve. My dad bought me supplies, and I left shortly after, promising to call when I arrived.

I called Miguel and Riley and had lunch with them before I left. I shared with them my decision to leave Hans and to take some time away from here. I asked for some space from Miguel to think, and he agreed. When I got to my aunt's, I literally passed out from exhaustion and stress.

The following morning, I quit my job at the bar without notice, explaining my situation to my boss. The next few days were spent trying to get Hans to understand that I needed time and space to think, despite his continuous attempts to contact me.

Hans was relentless. I eventually had to block his number. I just couldn't take the chance of him talking me into going back together, as I had done too many times, for far too long. From the very beginning, Hans had programed me so perfectly to say "Yes" to anything and everything he wanted me to do. But now it's time for me to start saying, "NO!"

Although first I needed to love myself again, to be able to feel again, to respect that person I had buried deep inside my soul, no matter what I had done or how far away I strayed from the person God wanted me to be.

30

Not an Easy Decision

After a few days at my aunt's, I knew with all my heart that I could not go back to Hans. I was desperate to have a man who truly loved me for me. I wanted to start a new chapter with Miguel, but I knew too that it was too soon to jump into something new.

I didn't know how to tell Hans about my decision to leave. So instead, I continued to tell him I hadn't made up my mind. To maintain some privacy, I got a pay-per-minute phone and used it to stay in touch with Miguel since Hans was monitoring our phone records online.

Miguel and I decided to take a break from all the stress over the past few months, and planned a weekend getaway to the beach.

However, since my parents were coming up that weekend, we had to postpone it for a few weeks.

On Saturday, I made dinner plans with my parents. When I heard the doorbell ring that afternoon, I thought it was my parents, so I opened the front door, but to my surprise, it was Hans. He said he knew we needed to talk, and also that I needed to have some maintenance work done on my car.

While I was at dinner with my family, Hans took care of the car, which I was grateful for, because he hadn't done that in a very long time. I explained to him that I was going to be staying with my parents, and that I would come back in a couple weeks to discuss my decision. Hans tried to hug me goodbye, but I stepped back and he got the message. Then we went our separate ways.

Going from working nonstop at the bar to not working at all was challenging for me. I started doing odds and ends to pass the time, but it wasn't the same. That's when I reached out to Miguel, and we decided to take our trip earlier than planned. I told my aunt I was going to visit my friends back in California so that Miguel and I could have some time alone.

On Friday, I picked him up after he finished work, and we headed to Santa Cruz. Except for me booking our hotel room, there was nothing else on our schedule for us to do or where to be. It was a glorious feeling to not have any agenda.

Over the next few days, it was so freeing to be away from our daily routines and the all drama back home. We both ignored our phones, except for letting my parents and his mom know that we were safe, and were simply enjoying each other's company.

It was the first time in a long time that I felt truly at peace and didn't want to return to my old life. But we knew eventually that we had to go back. The beach helped me clear my head and make a decision. And that decision was that I needed to go through with the divorce.

I dropped Miguel off at his mom's place and returned to Nevada to get my belongings. I let my parents know that I wanted to come back to California, but I wasn't totally sure how to go about it. That's when they offered me their support, without even one time saying, "I told you so," like I had feared they would.

They said they had an extra bedroom and that I could move in, and work as a janitor at my dad's office until I found a new job. They were both very concerned about me going to retrieve my things from Hans's place alone. That was when I reached out to my cousin Jeremiah who I knew I could count on to go with me. He gladly agreed to accompany me that weekend to get my stuff, and then join Hans and me in a discussion about the future.

This trip was especially meaningful to Jeremiah because he worked with an organization that helped girls who were victims of human trafficking rebuild their lives, and he felt that he would finally be able to help me escape my horrific situation.

While Hans was at work, Jeremiah and I went to Hans' trailer to collect my belongings. My mom and sister joined us to speed up the process. We each took a room and focused on just my stuff. I packed up all my clothes and personal belongings related to my past prior to meeting Hans.

I left everything on the walls, and I didn't take any furniture. And as much as I wanted to take my dogs with me, I didn't have a place for them, and I thought it would be easier for Hans if I left them both there with him. My plan was to gradually replace any of the household items that I needed. I didn't want to have anything that reminded me of what I had been through, so I left most everything else.

After eight very long and memorable years together, all I had to my name was my Honda, and all that I could fit in the front and back seat and in the trunk, along with my hopes for a better future.

After I dropped my things off at my parents' place, the time had finally come to have a final dinner with Hans. Even though I knew exactly what my decision would be, I still couldn't bring myself to tell him directly. I sat at the table, holding my sister's hand and shaking, trying to convey my choice through tears. Recognizing that I couldn't do it on my own, my cousin stepped in and informed Hans that I wanted an official divorce.

Of course, Hans didn't take it well. He kept asking me to

reconsider and promised to change, but I no longer believed him. He even tried to guilt-trip me by mentioning our "kids" and how I was "abandoning" them, knowing how much I loved our dogs. With that as his final attempt to make me stay, we headed to the parking lot and said a quick goodbye.

My sister and I got in the car, as Hans continued to speak with my cousin for a few more minutes. He asked my cousin to pray with him, which I interpreted as a last-ditch effort because Hans was not a religious person. But he knew I was, and so was my family.

At that moment, I knew I had made the right decision, even though getting him to sign the divorce papers would not be easy.

31

Signature Required

One day Hans showed up unannounced at my parents' house and asked if he could talk to me. It turned into a difficult situation, and there was tension in the air. My dad even felt the need to keep a loaded gun by his bedside because Hans just wouldn't go away. He continually tried to contact me and would stop by randomly without notice. To help ease the tension, I said I would call him, and he left without incident.

While we all sat in the backyard, my parents and I discussed the idea of me getting married again someday, and suddenly I remembered when Hans asked me to marry him; he said he had asked my dad for permission, but I never questioned it until now.

Out of curiosity, I asked my dad, "Did you ever give Hans your blessing for us to get married, if I left the profession I was in?"

With a shocked and surprised looked on his face, he answered, "Absolutely not! I would have never given him any such blessing!"

I knew deep in my heart it was true, and I was disappointed in Hans for lying about it because getting my dad's permission meant a lot to me, and until that moment I thought maybe I had it. However, now that the truth was out, I wasn't going to dwell on it. It's in the past where it needs to stay.

Eventually, I convinced Hans to meet me at a public restaurant to discuss and sign some papers related to our separation. My family and friends were there, keeping an eye on us at another table, because we didn't know what to expect. Hans tried to persuade me to change my mind, but I had already made up my mind.

We settled on what we would divide between us, and the only thing I asked for was a sentimental blanket my grandmother had made for me. I regretted leaving the dogs, but I believed they were better off with Hans. I knew he would never put them in harm's way.

The dinner was emotional but uneventful, and we agreed that the only communication between us would be about retrieving the blanket or handling court-related matters.

However, the divorce papers weren't as straightforward as we had hoped. We had to fill out additional paperwork and provide financial information. I noticed that Hans had misrepresented his employment status, which wasn't worth arguing about. I submitted the papers, and the waiting period began.

During this time, I was blessed with a job at a local shoe store and slowly started to rebuild my life. The stress was overwhelming, and Miguel, who was by this time officially my boyfriend, suggested we go to his hometown for a fundraiser. Meeting his friends made me nervous, but they turned out to be wonderful people. It was a refreshing experience, being myself without the weight of my past. Little did I know, I had made lifelong friends during that trip.

As my relationship with Miguel deepened, I spent more time at his place. It was hard to return to living with my parents after being independent for so long. Eventually, we decided to move in together, making our commitment official. So, I started looking for a new apartment. With the divorce papers finally in progress, and a date of termination of the marriage in sight, I felt ready to move on.

Miguel and I even got a puppy together, a cute Dachshund mix. This marked a new chapter in my life, and I was eager to embrace it. But maybe it wasn't quite time. God still had some work to do in us both before we could see how serious this relationship could be.

Miguel's roommate had informed him the next day that they would not be continuing the lease, so we figured why not get an apartment together. I mean we had already gotten a dog together, so we were pretty committed to being in a relationship anyway. So the plan was that Miguel would move in with his parents until we found a place.

It really felt like I was finally able to close the chapter on this chapter of my life and truly be able to move on but as it turned out, it would not be a smooth transition into a new life.

One night Miguel and I got into an argument, and he said, "I need some space and some time to figure things out before moving in with a girlfriend so quickly."

This crushed me, but luckily I had my parents and my puppy to comfort me. My dad poured me a glass of wine and just let me cry about how I thought this was the guy who would make things better, but damn if I was wrong again!

A few days later Miguel called and asked me to come to his parent's house to get the rest of the stuff I had left there. When I got there his mom Riley was out front waiting to talk to me.

"I need to give you a heads up, Amanda. Miguel has been a total wreck, and he so regrets ending things with you, but he doesn't know how to tell you," she explained, then continued. "Come in and try to stay calm, and give him a little space. Let him talk because his step dad had done this exact same thing to me in the past." So that's exactly what I did. About a hour into the visit he asked me to come back to his room and talk. He had to learn the harsh lesson in swallowing his pride.

Miguel sat down on the bed, and I sat in the chair. Then he asked sweetly, "Would you please come over here and sit next to me?" patting his hand on the bed. So I did, and he started apologizing and telling me that he was an idiot and almost lost the best girl he had ever met because he was scared of how serious things got so fast.

I started crying and he pulled me in so that I was lying on his chest. That's when he swore he would spend the rest of his life making it up to me because I didn't deserve to feel like this.

After a while, I told him I needed to go back to my parent's because I had to work the next morning, and I would text him when I got home.

My parents were relieved to see that I wasn't upset anymore, but they asked me to be careful not to get pressured into being with someone who wasn't ready to be in a committed relationship.

I so much appreciated their advice and their wisdom. I cannot predict the future, nor would I want to. But I was sure that what Miguel and I had was very special. And I wanted to see where it would go.

32

A New Lease on Life

A few months later, Miguel and I made the decision to move in together. I realize this may seem like a quick decision, but Miguel had helped me so much in this difficult transition to leave Hans, and he gave me the courage to do it, and it felt right for him to be in my life.

It didn't take long for us to find an apartment that we could afford. Granted it was not in the most favorable neighborhood, but it wasn't a trailer either. My parents helped me load up all the things I had been purchasing to fill my next place, and I headed out to start my new life. Even though the neighborhood was a little sketchy, I wasn't worried because Miguel was going to be living with me, which made me feel safe.

We soon became close with our neighbors and things just fell into place. I was blessed with a job at a temp agency and was quickly placed in an office. This meant that I didn't need to work at the shoe store anymore and was able to do part time at my dad's office.

The temp company said I was a great fit and ended up buying out my contract, and they permanently hired me as their receptionist. Miguel was working part time for his parents' company and things seemed to be falling into place nicely.

One day while I was at work, I received a phone call from Hans. He informed me that he was getting a job with a security company which would mean he would need to get his guards card and that meant passing a very extensive background check.

As part of the background check, they'd be calling me since we had been married, and he asked me to tell them he had never smoked marijuana, had never associated with criminals and to avoid talking about anything relating to the sex industry.

"Okay," I said, "we'll see if they really call me." And we hung up. Of course, they called me, and this was my chance to finally end his control over me.

I told the man on the phone that he had smoked marijuana when we were married, but I couldn't confirm anything recently. I also told him that Hans hung out around motorcycle clubs, and

I wouldn't be able to give a good character reference seeing as we had just gone through a nasty divorce. Which, of course, he had kind of expected that as my answer since the divorce date was still pending according to the court documents.

The man then informed me that Hans had listed my dad as another reference because of his military status, and I confirmed my dad's phone number. I cannot tell you exactly what their conversation entailed, but I can tell you when my dad called me afterwards, he couldn't believe that Hans had the audacity to think he was going to leave a good reference. He said he informed the man of my past career and told them how he thought I was manipulated by a predator, but that was all he was willing to share with me about their conversation.

Please don't get me wrong. I didn't want to ruin things for Hans, but I wanted to bring an end to his control over how I got to talk and act when I saw my chance.

Life for me carried on without any more communication from Hans and his family, thank God. Before I knew it, December had come, and I received the call from my mom that I had been waiting six months to get. She had in her hand a letter from the courts. I asked her to open it, and enclosed was my official divorce decree! Praise the Lord!

That was it! After eight very long years, it was all over! I could finally apply for my new driver's license and social security card and change my name back to my maiden name, ending this chapter of my life for good.

We all went out to dinner to celebrate, and it was one of the calmest and sweetest nights I had had in years. What a wonderful life it was going to be!

33

Dawn's New Light

By this time I was only working two nights a week at my dad's office, and phasing myself out of working two jobs since Miguel and I both had stable employment. It was wonderful to have a partner who was contributing more than just staying home to watch the dogs.

Life had finally settled down for us as we worked hard all week. Then on the weekends, Miguel and I would often relax at home or sometimes get together with my parents or my sisters so I could continue to repair the damage I had caused to those relationships when I was with Hans. It may take me a lifetime, but I'm ready to show them all how truly sorry I am for what I put them through. Thankfully, Miguel never had any issues with my family, and I was able to see them whenever I wanted.

One day my cousin Jeremiah called to let me know that he was volunteering with a local non-profit organization called Awaken that helped sex trafficked victims get out of that life and back on their feet. Jeremiah invited Miguel and me to join him in the walk that the organization was doing around the Sparks Marina to help bring awareness to their cause.

My cousin thought it could help me with the healing process I was going through if I saw the support systems that are out there and maybe even share my story to some of the people he was working with. So we agreed to come up that weekend and join him on the walk.

On the drive over the hill, I was super nervous and told Miguel I wasn't sure if I was ready to tell anyone that I had been in the sex industry for fear of being judged. It was still very hard for me to admit that I was in the same group of people as the victims this organization helped rescue.

When Miguel and I got to the Marina we met up with Jeremiah, and he introduced us to a few of his friends as "the cousin I told you about." They were all so kind. They even told me if I wanted to share any of my story that they'd be honored to listen. They also said if I wasn't ready for that yet, that it would be okay, too.

After much thought, I decided I just wasn't ready to share my story yet. Even though many of the things I had done in the past were not completely my idea, I put on a front that I was okay with it, unlike the girls who were kidnapped and forced into doing things.

One of the victims shared, "Sometimes as a defense mechanism, I would pretend to be okay with what was happening to me, and fake being proud of it as a way to hide the shame I felt inside." When I heard her say that it hit me like a knife in the heart. It was at that moment I realized my cousin was right and that I had indeed been sex trafficked.

I had misconstrued what sex trafficked actually meant and thought the sex industry meant that I wasn't a victim because I willingly did whatever I was told. However, I know in my heart, if it hadn't been for Hans, I would have NEVER gone into the sex industry on my own. It was not how I was raised.

Miguel stayed with me the rest of the afternoon walking around the Marina. Then we had an early dinner with Jeremiah and headed back over the hill for home. I was so grateful to Miguel for going with me and helping me to get through a rough day.

At my dad's office a few months later, they had brought in a psychologist to conduct a communication seminar for their business. When my dad found out that her main practice in Texas was focused on helping women who had faced difficult situations (like sex trafficking), he thought it would be a good idea for me to share my story with her.

He told her a little about my past and asked her to join me for lunch because he knew that, despite my tough exterior, I needed help coping with everything that had happened over the years. I agreed to have lunch with her the next day.

She had emailed me prior to lunch and asked me to jot down a quick timeline of events which had led me into the sex industry. I agreed, and in doing so, I was sent spiraling into a wave of emotion and was absolutely appalled when what I thought had taken years to happen had, in fact, only taken a few months.

I emailed her the timeline and waited to see what she had to say at lunch the next day. I was so thankful that music had always been a way to calm my anxiety, and I just started listening to Mandisa's song "Overcomer" again and again. This gave me the strength I needed not to let the timeline keep me upset for the rest of the night.

During our lunch, she said she couldn't believe how much I had been through in such a short time; to go from graduating with a 4.25 GPA, with hopes of attending a 4-year university, and trying out for the college track team, to a month later moving out and starting to strip. Then within four months I was making porn movies and had done it for years before moving into legal and illegal prostitution.

When we were getting ready to leave, she said most

emphatically, "If there's nothing else you take away from our conversation today, I want you to know this one thing. You are not a survivor of human trafficking. You are a thriver!" She never wanted me to forget that, and I know I never will.

She commended me for not succumbing to substance abuse despite the challenges I faced. She truly believed that my story could help someone else avoid a similar path, and encouraged me to start journaling my experiences as a healing exercise and possibly turn it into a book someday, with the hope that it might inspire others.

When I got home I told Miguel about all she had said, and he agreed it would be good to get it out of my head and on paper so that I could actually begin to move forward. This was when I started writing after work. Journalling definitely helped, but I knew I needed something more to actually heal.

I didn't feel the need to join any support groups because I was still concerned about how people would react when I told them what I used to be and do. Instead, I decided to write it all down and go from there. This was my therapy.

It got pretty intense at times, and on those nights, Miguel was there to comfort me. After several weeks of nonstop writing, I needed to take a break. Instead of writing after work, my mom taught me how to crochet. It was such a wonderful bonding experience for me because I knew I had missed out on so much when I was gone. Even my sister joined us.

I had only been divorced for a few weeks, and this would be my first Christmas without seeing Han's family. I'll admit that after eight years, I struggled a little not being around them. However, it also meant for the first time in years, I was able to attend Christmas Eve service at my parent's church with them! This was something I had wanted to do for years, but Hans was so against going, so I never pushed the issue.

Miguel was happy to go to church with us, and when we got back to my parents, we all changed into our pajamas and watched the holiday classic "It's a Wonderful Life." When it was over, Miguel and I went back to our apartment.

The next morning we went to Miguel's parents for breakfast and opened presents. Then back to my parent's for presents and dinner.

My heart was so full and overjoyed being able to see my family for the holidays without being on edge waiting for a fight that I knew was coming. I finally had peace and calm during this beautiful season for the first time in almost eight years.

It took Miguel and I a few years to understand the concept that God needed to be our foundation if we were going to do this the right way.

This was especially hard for Miguel to understand because he wasn't raised in a Christian home, and it took him a while before he could fully commit. But in 2016, that was exactly what he did! I was so proud of him.

I, too, had business to do with God, and I rededicated my life to Him as well in 2016, when Miguel and I were baptized together.

With my past now behind me, I was so ready to make all things right again. It was a glorious day in 2018, when Miguel asked me to be his wife, and I gladly and eagerly accepted.

Miguel and I were married in 2019, and we are committed to our journey together. We've had our share of ups and downs, but every day it gets better. We started out being two young people who didn't know what we were doing, yet we knew with all our hearts that we wanted a life together.

Today we are homeowners, and we have two beautiful children, a little girl and a sweet baby boy, and two dogs. We find ourselves constantly surrounded by both of our families and good friends who support us in being the best versions of ourselves. We've even discovered an amazing church to be a part of, as we continue to grow closer to what God wants and allowing Him to guide us through this unpredictable world.

Now I'm finally ready to write my life story in the sincere hopes that it will touch someone's life and help prevent them from following the same challenging path that I did.

Don't get me wrong, life hasn't been all sunshine and roses since letting go of my past, but I've never considered returning to that old lifestyle, not even once.

Every experience I went through has shaped me into the strong, independent woman I am today. However, I do wonder on occasion what life would have been like had I chose a different path. But then I remember Miguel.

Would we still have met had I not chosen Hans? I don't know. But I am so blessed that Miguel came along when he did and rescued me, and eventually gave me the strongest reason to help others steer clear of the sex industry, my daughter.

So, I say clearly and emphatically to all of you who want to stop trying to get out of the nightmare situation you are in. DO NOT GIVE UP! Don't let the dark clouds over your head define the end of your dreams.

I can attest that no matter how dark and lonely life may feel, there is a reason for everything we go through. If you made bad choices or decisions, it's not too late to change your mind.

God has a reason for everything, and although it may not seem like it right now, one day you will see the reason. It may take days, weeks or even years, but trust me when I say, "You will see it someday!"

There is nothing that you have done that you can't ask God to forgive, and to help you forgive yourself. Like the Bible says in 1 John 1:9, *"If we confess our sins, He is faithful and righteous to forgive us our sins and to cleanse us from all unrighteousness."*

This is my story, and if any part of it resonates with you, it means that you are the reason for me writing it. It is a calling that I embrace with all my heart.

The scars I carry are both physical and emotional, a testament to the unimaginable pain that can be inflicted upon the most vulnerable among us.

But today, I stand before you not just a survivor, but a thriver, a warrior, a beacon of hope for those who still suffer in silence.

Suffer no more, my friend. You deserve to find your happiness too.

Do not let anyone tell you that you can't, because you can! It's not too late for you to have an amazing life, the life you were always meant to live!

Stay strong and determined. And please don't give up! There's a beautiful new life waiting for you!

35

Statistics

Adjusted for population, Nevada's commercial sex market is by far the largest of any state.

At least 5,016 individuals are sold for sex in an average month in Nevada. Nevada's number of prostituted persons per capita is 63% larger than the next largest state of New York, and more than twice as many as in California.

Legalized prostitution appears to have done nothing to stem victimization within the illicit sex trade — the data in the study show that prostituted persons in the illegal trade around licensed brothels are at a similar risk of having been trafficked as those in areas without legal brothels.

More than 13% of Nevada prostituted persons are advertised under the age of 21.

More than 1 out of every 10 prostituted persons in Nevada is too young to buy alcohol. These young individuals are almost twice as likely to "travel" while being prostituted compared to those who are 21 and older.

Many prostituted persons are advertised for their youth, regardless of their stated age. For example, phrases like "fresh meat," "brand new" and "daddy's little girl" are all used to connote the youth of sex workers.

Youth is an important characteristic sought by sex buyers in Nevada.

Evidence of the importance of youth to sex buyers in Nevada comes from the advertised prices of young, prostituted persons. The data show higher prices are charged for younger females in Nevada.

The data put Nevada in the top ten states in the country in terms of youth of prostituted persons.

This study was commissioned by Awaken and research was funded by the Nebraska Women's Foundation of Omaha. Study design, data collection, and analyses were devised and implemented independently by HTI. Several outside reviewers gave commendations of the report. The research team retained full and exclusive authority in deciding whether and how to respond to comments from outside reviewers, and as such is fully and solely responsible for the report's findings and interpretations.

Awaken Nevada INC is a faith-based non-profit organization on a mission to eradicate commercial sexual exploitation. With a focus on providing housing, education, and holistic restoration services, we stand shoulder-to-shoulder with survivors, giving them the tools they need to reclaim their lives and build brighter futures.

UPDATE APRIL 2018:

"Backpage.com and affiliated websites have been seized as part of an enforcement action by the Federal Bureau of Investigation, the U.S. Postal Inspection Service, and the Internal Revenue Service Criminal Investigation Division, with analytical assistance from the Joint Regional Intelligence Center."

GLOBAL STATISTICS

The International Labour Organization (ILO) estimates that more than 40 million people around the world were victims of modern slavery in 2016.

At any given time in 2016, 4.8 million people were victims of forced sexual exploitation. On average, they are held for 23.4 months in their situation before escaping or being freed. The vast majority are women and girls. Children represent more than 20%

of the victims.

ILO estimates that annual profits per victim of sexual exploitation is $21,800.

The United Nations Office on Drugs and Crime (UNODC) notes that children make up almost a third of all human trafficking victims worldwide and women and girls comprise 71 percent of human trafficking victims.

UNODC estimates the total market value of illicit human trafficking at 32 billion US dollars.

NATIONAL STATISTICS

More than 31,600 total cases of human trafficking have been reported to the National Human Trafficking Hotline in the last eight years. The Hotline receives an average of 100 calls per day.

One out of every three adolescents on the street will be lured toward prostitution within 48 hours of leaving home according to the National Incidence Studies of Missing, Abducted, Runaway, and Thrownaway Children.

The National Runaway Switchboard estimates that on any given night there are approximately 1.3 million homeless youth living unsupervised on the streets, in abandoned buildings, with friends, or with strangers. Homeless youth are at a higher risk for physical abuse, sexual exploitation, mental health disabilities, substance abuse, and death.

In 2016, an estimated one out of six endangered runaways reported to the National Center for Missing and Exploited Children were likely child sex trafficking victims. Of those, 86 percent were in the care of social services or foster care when they ran.

Several studies have found that 50 to 72 percent of women in street prostitution have experienced severe violence at the hands of buyers, pimps/traffickers, and police officers.

A report from the U.S. Department of Justice and the Urban Institute found that pimps surveyed from eight major U.S. cities cited making anywhere between $5,000 to $32,833 per week.

HUMAN TRAFFICKING DATA Activities, 2023

NCJ Number 307345

Date Published October 2023

Publication Series Human Trafficking Data Collection

Activities Description

This report details ongoing and completed efforts to measure and analyze the nationwide incidence of human trafficking, to describe characteristics of human trafficking victims and offenders, and to describe criminal justice responses to human trafficking offenses. The report provides information on human trafficking suspects referred to and prosecuted by U.S. attorneys, human trafficking defendants convicted and sentenced to federal prison, and admissions to state prison for human trafficking.

HIGHLIGHTS

A total of 2,027 persons were referred to U.S. attorneys for human trafficking offenses in fiscal year 2021, a 49% increase from the 1,360 persons referred in 2011.

The number of persons prosecuted for human trafficking more than doubled from 2011 to 2021 (from 729 persons to 1,672 persons, respectively).

Of the 1,197 defendants charged in federal court for human trafficking offenses in fiscal year 2021, 92% were male and 60% were white. Of the 201 defendants charged with peonage, slavery, forced labor, and sex trafficking in fiscal year 2021, 77% were male and 58% were black.

At year-end 2021, 1,657 persons were in the custody of a state prison serving a sentence for a human trafficking offense.

36

~~~

Amanda's Life Timeline

November 1988

I was born to unwed teenage parents, who married the following summer.

June 9, 1990

We moved to California.

2002

I started high school.

2003

I started dating Justin for three years.

2005

Started my senior year of high school.

2006

Joined high school track team. Met Coach Hans.

2006

Left Justin and was secretly dating Hans as a senior in high school. (I agreed to an open relationship without knowing what it meant.)

2006

I enrolled into Sacramento State.

January 2007

I moved out of my parents' house and in with Hans.

February 2007

Tried an amateur night at a strip club and ended up getting a job there.

March 2007

I dropped out of Sacramento State.

June 2007

I started filming movies and working part time at the strip club.

December 2007

Cohosted the Miss Nude Canada Pageant in Toronto, Canada.

January 2008

I went full-time into making movies and cohosting a radio talk show.

May 2008

Moved to Los Angeles, CA with Hans.

July 2008

Moved back to Sacramento, with Hans.

September 2008

I agreed to become the submissive partner to Hans, and it eventually resulted in him physically "punishing" me for misbehaving/embarrassing him in public.

January 2009

I commuted to L.A. for work every two weeks.

April 2009

I was sexually assaulted.

May 2009

Went back part-time to filming because of our living expenses.

June 2009

I started working at the Bunny Ranch in Carson City, NV.

June-July 2009

Continued filming and working at the Ranch part time.

October 2009

Hans and I were engaged.

July 2010

I married Hans. (My immediate family and 95% of extended family refused to come.)

October 2010

I had a chemical pregnancy.

October 2010-May 2011

I worked with Serenity doing privates (prostitution from home).

July 2011

I got a "normal job" and started bartending.

July 2012

Found out I was pregnant.

October 2012

I miscarried and had my first surgery (D&C).

October 27, 2012

We moved from a beautiful house into a trailer.

October 2012 - February 2013

Started falling into a depression.

December 2012 - February 2013

Agreed to a "wife swap" trying to save my marriage and it resulted in my husband dating the other wife.

February 2013

I finally left my husband.

March 2013

I officially started dating Miguel.

October 2013

Started my first full-time office job.

December 2013

I was officially divorced from Hans.

July 2016

Rededicated my life to Jesus.

March 2018

Miguel and I were engaged.

November 2019

Miguel and I were married.

February 2020

We bought a house.

September 2020

My sweet daughter was born.

July 2023

My baby boy was born.

January 2024

My book was published.

Made in the USA
Las Vegas, NV
19 January 2024